LOTUS IN THE FIRE

What is my own Buddha-mind?
Upon enlightenment the lotus
will blossom in a roaring fire
and endure throughout eternity.

—Zen master Bassui

LOTUS
in the FIRE

The Healing Power
of Zen

JIM BEDARD

SHAMBHALA
Boston & London
1999

SHAMBHALA PUBLICATIONS, INC.
Horticultural Hall
300 Massachusetts Avenue
Boston, Massachusetts 02115
http://www.shambhala.com

© 1999 by Jim Bedard

9 8 7 6 5 4 3 2 1

FIRST EDITION
Printed in the United States of America

♾ This edition is printed on acid-free paper that meets
the American National Standards Institute Z39.48 Standard.
Distributed in the United States by Random House, Inc.,
and in Canada by Random House of Canada Ltd.

LIBRARY OF CONGRESS CATALOGING-IN-PUBLICATION DATA
Bedard, Jim.
    Lotus in the fire: the healing power of Zen / Jim Bedard.—1st ed.
      p. cm.
    ISBN 1-57062-430-5 (alk. paper)
    1. Bedard, Jim. 2. Religious life—Zen Buddhism.
    3. Healing—Religious aspects—Zen Buddhism. 4. Acute myelocytic leukemia—Patients—Canada—Biography.
    5. Spiritual biography—Canada. I. Title.
    BQ942.E37A3 1999   98-31120
    294.3′4442—dc21   CIP

For Sensei Sunyana Graef

Thank you for your love, guidance, and support.
I will be forever grateful.

CONTENTS

PREFACE

Sunday, August 27, 1995

"How serious is it?"

"You have less than two weeks to live, Mr. Bedard." I had asked for the straight goods, and this was the doctor's response to my question. The diagnosis was leukemia, and he suspected it was an acute type, since it was progressing so rapidly.

The night before, my wife, Margaret, and I had gone to emergency at a hospital in Peterborough, near our home in Bethany, Ontario, to have some minor swelling of my hands and ankles checked. There had been a fatal car accident not long after we were admitted, and the waiting room was chaotic. As the family of the accident victims arrived, the situation deteriorated. These people, I felt, needed immediate attention; I was embarrassed to be taking the doctors' time for what I assumed was no more than an allergic reaction to something I had ingested. I got up to leave, thinking I could always return in a few days. But Margaret urged me to stay. We had already been there for hours, and our doctor, too, had been patiently waiting with us. She felt it would be inconsiderate to leave while he waited by himself for the test results. Within the week we realized that had I left that night without waiting to hear the diagnosis, I might never have lived long enough to return.

The test results finally came back: I had a serious bone marrow disorder but could return home for the evening. I was to contact the doctor if I felt worse. That night I called my family with the news, trying not to alarm them until we knew for certain that it was indeed serious. My mother and my sister Shirley-Anne decided to come to Bethany early the next morning anyway. By noon my ankles were extremely swollen and I felt listless. When I called my doctor, he insisted on seeing me immediately. He ordered a blood sample and told me to go at once to St. Michael's Hospital in Toronto, about an hour and a half away.

My energy was failing. Margaret, my mother, and Shirley-Anne grew concerned. On that summer Sunday afternoon, traffic was crawling on all lanes of the 401 heading into Toronto. Desperate to get to the hospital quickly, my sister, who was driving, put on the flashers and swerved onto the shoulder, where we traveled most of the way. When we arrived at the hospital, I was immediately admitted, answered a lot of questions, and underwent some very thorough tests.

That evening the doctor came into my room and confirmed that I had leukemia and that it was moving fast. From the looks on the faces of Margaret, my mother, and Shirley-Anne, I could tell that the prognosis was not good. Could I really be that sick? Although I felt a little weak, I did not feel sick enough to be facing a serious and life-threatening illness.

It all seemed unreal. Only a few days earlier I had been cutting logs and splitting wood with three of my closest friends at our cabin near Algonquin Provincial Park, Ontario. Randy, Ross, Ian, and I often traveled to that area to spend time canoeing, hiking, and meditating. We had been friends for fifteen years and through our common interest in Zen Buddhism had gone to numerous Zen retreats together.[1] In 1993 we had decided to purchase land and build a cabin on the Madawaska River. Through several weeks and many weekends of hard labor, the cabin finally took shape; it was an expression of the close affection we felt for each other. That weekend in August was the first time we had allowed ourselves shorter work periods at the cabin, giving us extra time to enjoy the property and one another's company.

Our first afternoon went by quickly as we cleared trees, cut logs for firewood, and carried them up a steep hill to the cabin. I was used to hard physical labor. I've always had energy to spare. On this afternoon I felt tired from the work, but so did everyone else. That evening we went for an invigorating swim in the Madawaska River and then sat down to Ross's not-so-famous vegetarian chili and rice. As we watched the sunset, I remember saying that days this wonderful were few and far between. Then a remarkable thing happened. While we watched the setting sun, a large meteor streaked across the sky. We followed it for several seconds before it disappeared over the horizon. It was as big as the full moon and had a green and turquoise tail at least ten times as long as its diameter. The meteor had barely faded from sight when the northern lights appeared, dancing in a way I had never seen before. It was, without a doubt, one of the most extraordinary evenings of my life.

Now, here I was, less than a week later, asking the doctor if the two weeks I had booked off from work for treatment would be sufficient. He looked at Margaret and Shirley-Anne as if he were getting permission to give it to me straight once more. With their nod of approval he tilted his head to one side, raised his eyebrows, looked me in the eye, and said, "Jim, we hope you're still going to be with us in two weeks." I thought about that for a moment. It still didn't seem real. I was forty-two years old, with four kids, a good career, and my life ahead of me. I did not feel sick enough to be facing such a serious prognosis. Perhaps it was a mistake? Years before I had been sent to my doctor after attempting to do-nate blood. I was immediately tested for both internal bleeding and leukemia because it appeared that my blood counts were so low. However, it turned out that someone had mistakenly typed in the wrong information at the blood donor clinic. I was in perfectly good health after all. Margaret and I joked about that first diagnosis with my doctor. Our eyes and hearts were asking, "Are you really sure?"

The bone marrow aspiration the next morning was conclusive. It was AML—acute myeloid leukemia.

"Doc," I asked, "I had a friend who suffered for months from bone cancer, and the treatment made him tremendously nauseated. In the end, he died weak and in terrible pain. Wouldn't it be best for me to take some time while I still feel healthy and spend it with my wife, children, and friends. What would I be risking? Do you really think it's that serious? What if I decide not to have chemotherapy immediately—I'd like to explore some alternative treatment options—how much time do you think I would have?"

"You'd have about seven to ten days to live," he replied. "And Jim, don't kid yourself. There will not be a good day among them."

"Well, then," came my response, "let's get on with it."

LOTUS IN THE FIRE

1

LETTING GO

Nothing seems
So transient as
Human life:
The dew on the petal
Of the morning glory.

—JAPANESE WAKA POEM

Monday, August 28

THE BONE MARROW ASPIRATION I underwent on that Monday morning was the first of many I would face in the next several months. It was an extremely painful test. During this procedure a thick, threaded needle was "screwed" into the pelvic bone just below the waist near the spine. The skin and flesh in the area were numbed, but the pelvic bone and marrow were not. When the physician drew back the needle to withdraw the marrow sample, I felt acute pain for several minutes. Some doctors were more experienced than others, and some aspirations went better than others. In the coming months I would undergo bone marrow aspirations and lumbar punctures on both ends of the pain spectrum.

The night before, after everyone had left, I had contemplated my situation. In the hospital, night is a good time for serious re-flection. The days are busy with doctors and nurses taking a multi-tude of tests and with visits from the cleaning staff, kitchen help, and of course, friends and family. But night, like death, must be faced alone.

Am I really dying? I thought. *What will it be like? Why is it I haven't known this all along? Surely I must have always known that I was going to die. Even if I beat this thing I will inevitably be facing death again in the near future or many years from now. But for certain, I am going to die.* The awareness of the inevitability of my own death hit me in a way I cannot de-scribe. It was as if I had discovered some secret truth about exis-tence that no one knew. I felt a compulsive urge to let everyone else know about this great realization.

For years I had been practicing Zen meditation—sitting, or zazen—a discipline of "letting go" of formations of consciousness. Whenever I was able to drop old habits of thought, I felt a sense of liberation and was inspired to continue practicing, to return again and again to the meditation cushion.

Now as I lay awake in the hospital, I was dealing with the ulti-mate letting go, beyond anything I had faced on the mat. Was I prepared to say good-bye to my four children, my wife, my Zen teacher, my friends, my family? This letting go was for real.

How I wished I had done more sitting when healthy, spent more time contemplating the transient nature of life. I realized deep in my bones how important it was never to waste a moment. Life is so precious and so frail.

I thought about the inscription on the han:[1]

> Great is the matter of birth and death.
> Life slips quickly by,
> Time waits for no one.
> Wake up! Wake up!
> Don't waste a moment.

Yes, indeed, great is the matter of birth and death! At Zen retreats, I was sometimes asked to give short talks. I often urged people to reflect on that verse. "Soon," I'd say, "we will all be faced with the truth of impermanence. Do not take refuge in this transient body. The inevitability of our own death cannot be denied. It is imperative not to waste a moment!" My own admonitions echoed in my mind. I realized how much spiritual work there was left for me to do, and death, at this very moment, was at my doorstep.

Here in the silence of my hospital room, near midnight, my racing, confused thoughts began to settle, and as they did, I became aware of a surprising clarity of mind. I reflected more calmly on what had taken place that day. *If I have to die,* I thought, *at least let me do it "right," with my mind at peace.* I did not want to die afraid, or as one great Zen master put it, "with arms and legs grasping to hold on, like a crab thrown into boiling water." This was certainly the time for me to get it right. If not now, when? I had asked myself this question many times while healthy at Zen retreats. But it's one thing to contemplate death when in good health, quite another to face it for real. There was no way to dodge the issue now. It was time to look death directly in the face and get to work on the essential. I remembered the words of Zen master Bassui, "If you carry on your Zen practice faithfully, even while dying, you will unquestionably achieve enlightenment in your next existence."

All beings will someday be faced with a similar situation, I thought. *How many will be ready?* Many times I had heard my Zen teacher say how absurd it was that so many people seemed to live as if only others were going to die. In the months that followed this night in the hospital, I would meet many individuals who were not prepared to face the inevitable. My heart went out to them.

As I sat alone in my bed, and in silence, a wonderful feeling came over me. It was *gratitude.* I was astonished to find this unbidden yet welcome guest. I felt so grateful to have found a spiritual practice in this life and so grateful to have spent fifteen years practicing letting go. Tears came to my eyes. I placed my hands together and made a weak but heartfelt bow to all those who had carried the Buddha's teaching to this present day.[2]

In my hospital bed, I wanted to do a chanting service and could feel the vibrations of past chanting ceremonies in my whole being.[3] "Chanting has the power to penetrate seen and unseen realms," my first teacher, Roshi Philip Kapleau, often said. It is truly a powerful practice. I had turned to chanting that very first night when I returned home from the Peterborough hospital with swollen hands and legs and the news that I was critically ill. I knew that chanting would help me more than anything else in dealing with my overwhelming thoughts and emotions. Margaret and I had hugged our children especially warmly and said good night to them. She then went next door to speak with a friend, and I entered my meditation room. I turned toward the Buddha on the altar and made a bow. Normally I would begin a chanting service with three prostrations. That night, though, there were no prostrations. My legs were too swollen and I was tiring too quickly. Instead, I made standing bows, then sat down on my mat and began a chanting service.[4]

> Form here is only Emptiness,
> Emptiness only form . . .
> no feeling, thought, or choice,
> nor is there consciousness . . .
> nor even act of sensing.
> No withering, no death . . .
> So know that the bodhisattva,
> holding to nothing whatever
> but dwelling in prajña wisdom,
> is freed of delusive hindrance,
> rid of the fear bred by it,
> and reaches clearest nirvana.

I chanted for some time. I was reluctant to leave the little meditation room, as I did not know when I might have the opportunity to sit there again. I had spent intimate hours in it with friends, my teacher, and my children, and many, many more hours sitting there alone in silence. The words of the chant filled my heart and mind.

This first night in the hospital, as I lay alone in my bed, I didn't have the energy to chant. It had been a long day, and the stress of all that had taken place was beginning to take its toll. Wondering how much pain awaited me, I again placed my hands palm-to-palm in *gassho* and resolved to greet my leukemia with gratitude for whatever teachings it would bring. I further promised myself that as I began my journey through this next period of my life, I would not get miserable or angry with anyone. It was my *karma*,[5] and an opportunity to expiate this karma was presenting itself.

"Let me find the strength," I prayed, "to make the most of this opportunity. I must find the courage that it will take for me to face this challenge with an open heart and with acceptance." I then prayed that the wisdom of the Buddha's teachings would not fail me. "If you don't let the dharma down, the dharma will not let you down" was the admonition I had heard a thousand times.[6]

With hands still pressed palm-to-palm I said in a loud whisper, "Great bodhisattvas, help me to be strong, lest others lose faith in the dharma. Please, forget not your ancient vows."[7]

I lay back exhausted and went to sleep.

Now, on this bright Monday morning in August, Margaret, Shirley-Anne, and my mom arrived, smiling. They told me that the other members of the family had been notified and would be coming soon.

I spent the rest of that day greeting brothers and sisters and their spouses, aunts, uncles, and some close friends. Most difficult of all was facing our four children.

"Margaret, do the kids know yet?" I asked that morning. I knew that this would be terrifying for them. There was no way to break the news gently. My children were already too familiar with leukemia, having lost their maternal grandmother to acute myeloid leukemia just a few years earlier.

"I called them last night and told them you had leukemia, but we didn't know then that it was AML. I'll tell them once they get here," Margaret replied. Margaret felt it was best if the children heard about it directly from her, and she wanted to be with them at the time. She was dreading it.

The night before, when Margaret had picked up the phone to call the children, she had thought, *This isn't going to be easy. How will I ever tell them?*

Amanda, sixteen, had answered the phone, and Margaret asked her to have eleven-year-old Raymond, our youngest, pick up the extension. They were spending the night with some friends near our home in Bethany.

"Hi kids . . . I'm in Toronto at St. Michael's Hospital with your father . . . he's . . . very sick. I'm not sure when I'll get home," she had told them, trying to sound calm.

"What's wrong with Dad?"

"He has leukemia."

"What! Leukemia?" Both Amanda and Raymond had burst into tears. Amanda had quickly hung up the phone and run downstairs to be with Raymond, who was sobbing uncontrollably.

"No, Mom, no! Oh no!" Raymond shouted.

Margaret had tried to reassure them by saying that there were many types of leukemia and that we did not yet know the long-term prognosis.

"Gee, Mom," Amanda said, sobbing, "Dad looked a little sick but not like he had cancer or anything serious."

"Try not to worry too much, honey. We really don't know how serious it is yet. I'll call you as soon as we know more."

Margaret had then called Jason, our eldest, and Bradley, who was thirteen. They were home, and when they heard the news they too had become distraught.

"It's got to be a mistake, Mom. There's no way Dad is that sick," said Jason.

"It's a little confusing for all of us, Jay. We'll know more tomorrow after the bone marrow aspiration," she said. "Jill will pick up Amanda and Ray in the morning and then bring you all in to the hospital."

Our neighbor Jill was a blessing. Over time, she made many three-hour round trips from Bethany to the hospital with the children, always arriving with fruit, sandwiches, and drinks for the family.

When the children arrived on that first visit, Margaret met with them privately and told them I had acute myeloid leukemia. When they realized the severity of the illness, they all burst into tears.

"There are many new treatments these days that did not exist even a few years ago," Margaret told them. "Remember that your dad is in much better shape and a lot younger than your grandmother was. Please kids, try not to be too upset in front of Dad, as he is really concerned about how you're all doing with this."

When they came into my room I could tell they were being careful not to show how overwrought they were. I almost broke down myself at one point but made my way to the washroom for a few minutes so that they would not see my tears. I did not want them any more afraid or upset than they already were.

At one point Amanda sensed that Raymond was about to lose it. She swooped him up and said, "Dad, we're going down to the cafeteria for a hot chocolate. Be back in a few minutes." They then found an empty lounge and, hugging each other, broke into tears. They never did get to that hot chocolate, but I was none the wiser.

As my relatives arrived from out of town, we did the usual catching up and told a few jokes. Then the reality of why we were together would hit us, and everyone would fall silent. I kidded that it might be our last chance for a family portrait. We took some pictures, joked a little, and hugged a lot.

"Please help me do this without any negativity," I asked my family. "In the short time I've been here I've heard visitors of other patients complaining to the nurses about trivial things. Please, let's not make this difficult for the staff. I'm sure they're doing their very best."

They all gave their word. My advice had been timely because with all the guests and relatives arriving to see me, the nurses were becoming inundated with inquiries about my condition. My eldest brother, Eric, tried to organize things a little: Margaret and a family representative were designated to meet with medical staff and keep the others informed. Eric quickly went to work on the staff. "What can I do to help? How would you like us to organize the visits? Please let us know if we're causing too much disruption." He made sure the nurses were often treated to late-night pastries and coffee.

One day there were more than twenty people in the hall waiting to see me. A nurse came into my room and asked jokingly if I were some kind of celebrity. Smiling, I replied that it was just that I was from a large Catholic family.

My energy was so low that there was no way I could continue to visit with everyone. The doctors told my family that it was very important for me to get some rest. My brothers stepped in to help out.

My youngest brother, Michael, decided to stand guard at my door. (He had recently broken his elbow and was wearing a sling. To this day when I go to a clinic and meet a nurse or doctor whom I haven't seen since my first round of chemotherapy, they will remember me if I tell them I was the one with the wounded sentinel at my door.) After monitoring visits all day long, Michael told the family that he would stay behind for a while and they could go ahead back to the hotel. Shirley-Anne left, then returned to check on Michael—she suspected he was having a hard time—and found him collapsed on the floor outside my room sobbing un-controllably. She tried to console him, telling him that being strong for the family did not mean he had to try to hide his own grief.

Tuesday, August 29

The next day, Tuesday morning, Margaret and I discussed funeral arrangements in great detail, as well as other pressing concerns such as our children's university expenses. We were fortunate that in Canada the national health system would take care of all our medical expenses. Nevertheless, there were other financial con-cerns. My disability insurance would cover our household ex-penses, and Margaret's income as a dietary assistant would cover groceries. Even so, it would be tight. I asked my office to send documents detailing life insurance policies and sick benefits. I also signed a living will and legal documents making my wife executor of our affairs. Margaret noticed that my energy was dwindling quickly, and she would have preferred that we spend quality time together. My concerns seemed premature to family and friends, but I think I was responding to a deep intuition. I needed to settle these matters and get them off my mind.

When they were with me, my family put on a good front. It was only much later that I learned of all the tears they shed in rooms down the hall. They were sympathetic and understanding, doing a remarkable job of finding a balance between allowing me time to talk about my dilemma and just being there to help me take my mind off things when I needed to. Sometimes we would say nothing, just sitting together quietly.

My closest friends from the Toronto Zen Centre—Ian, Randy, and Ross—came to visit. We set up an altar in my room with the Buddha figure from my home zendo[8] and some smaller figures that were given to me as gifts by my teacher and her family. We posted a Do Not Disturb sign on the door and began a chanting service using the *keisu* and *mokugyo* my friends had brought to the hospital. The staff was very accommodating, and we were able to have several chanting sessions together. Friends and family members who practiced Zen Buddhism also used one of the quiet rooms to do some chanting on my behalf when I was not up to it. Others in my family who once teased me about such practices soon developed a great respect for chanting when they saw what a positive effect it had.

Early that afternoon Sunyana-sensei, a Zen Buddhist priest and for the past year my teacher and the spiritual director of our center, came to visit from her home in Vermont.[9] A month earlier I had written her requesting to be accepted as a disciple. For me, becoming her disciple meant deepening my commitment to the dharma. It was also a way to actualize my lifelong commitment to my teacher. She told me at the time that we had not worked together long enough for me to make such a serious commitment and asked that I wait another year before bringing it up again. I responded by sending her a letter saying that I respected her decision and that I would make my request again the following year. Then I asked her to promise me that if I should die before having the opportunity to request once more to become her disciple, she would perform the disciple ceremony standing by my body or with my ashes.

As soon as our eyes met Sensei said, "Did you have a premonition about this?" I don't know whether I did or not, but it was the only time in my life I recall having written about my own death.

Since my first day of introduction to the Buddhist teaching, I had dreamed of someday becoming a disciple. Sunyana-sensei could read in my eyes and my heart that I was concerned that I might never have the opportunity to do so in this life. She asked, "Would you still like to go ahead with the ceremony? We can do it now if you wish."

"Perhaps it would be better to wait," I replied. "It will give me something to look forward to." Then I thought, *I really would rather do this ceremony in the flesh.* I prayed that I would live to see that day.

The truth was that I had no sense of whether or not I would live to see the next day. I lost all sense of time. There was just this "now," and I was attempting to make the most of each and every moment. At the same time, my energy was failing fast. Lying there I thought, *Was it just the night before last that I was thinking I wasn't sick enough to be dying?*

My visits were cut short and I began to appreciate even more the help from my family in answering phone calls and meeting friends.

Later that day I was taken down to the operating room to have a Hickman catheter inserted into my heart for the chemotherapy treatments. Arm veins are not used, as they can collapse from the heavy toxic doses of drugs. It was going to be risky because my platelet count was so low. The surgeon wanted to wait until I had received more platelet infusions, but my hematologist insisted that the catheter be inserted immediately. It would take several days for the chemotherapy to begin to take effect. The leukemia was advancing quickly and they were racing against time.

As I was wheeled out of the room for surgery, I was greeted by a sight at once comical and inspiring. My friends and relatives lined the hall and stood with arms extended, making a victory fist. It was something right out of a Billy Jack movie from the seventies. I began to laugh heartily. The nurses and my porter shook their heads, wondering if we were all a little nuts, but they laughed too. With that, the whole ordeal became a bit less frightening.

To have a catheter inserted into the heart, only local anesthetic is used. The area from the collarbone to the breast is numbed, the most painful part of the procedure. The surgeon made two small incisions in my chest, the first at the base of the neck near the collarbone. Here the catheter was inserted into a large vein and threaded through this vein until it reached the large vessel to the heart. The other end of the catheter is threaded under the skin and brought out through a second incision, the exit site, just next to my right nipple. The procedure was quite painless once the local anesthetic took, but there was much discomfort as the large needle was pulling the catheter from the neck through to the chest under the skin. I felt sick to my stomach as the surgeon pulled the needle from the breast, attempting to feed the catheter from the collarbone to the exit site. Several times my shoulder and chest left the table from the force of his pulling.

Once it was done, I was grateful to have the Hickman line replace the intravenous needles in my arms. In my case the "line" consisted of one catheter extending from the heart with two lines leading into it. This way I could receive blood products and medications at the same time. If a line were not in use it would be capped immediately to prevent air from getting into the heart. For me, though, both lines were always active. These lines provided a painless route for receiving blood products, medications, or nutritional supplements. It also made it possible for blood samples to be taken without discomfort.

Over the next few weeks I was trained in caring for the lines and the exit site. I was told to keep the exit site sterile. Infections are common in that area and can pose a serious threat once chemotherapy depletes the white blood cells, which fight infection. I was also cautioned that air must never get too far into the line. If I saw any air, I must immediately clamp the line and turn onto my left side. That way the air would harmlessly disperse. Turning onto my right side, however, could be fatal, as it would force air into my heart, possibly causing cardiac arrest.

The surgery went well, but there was a lot of bleeding. My platelets were low and my white blood cells had hit rock bottom. It was going to be close. I had been given only two weeks to live; I had already been in the hospital three days; and the chemotherapy would take several days to be effective. We all wondered whether the chemotherapy would begin to work in time to catch the racing leukemia cells. I was declining fast, and my body had little reserve to fight off infections. When I returned to my room, the chemo was administered, and I immediately felt weak and nauseated. I was told it is often the first round of chemotherapy that is toughest to take.

I was still feeling sore from the bone marrow aspiration the day before. The numbness was wearing off in my chest and I was beginning to feel discomfort there as well. *This is not going to be easy,* I thought. *Will I have the strength to do this the way I want to? Where will I find the courage to face all the pain and discomfort?* I was only a few days into it and already I was looking for a break.

So much of what had seemed important to me only days before now seemed meaningless: worries that the company I worked for would be sold, loan payments, and a mortgage that was not going to be paid off for years. The normal stresses of everyday life seemed dim in comparison with the challenge I was facing. Realizing my own impermanence and the transience of all things, I felt an acute sense of urgency. Yet paralleling this was a feeling of peace, a feeling of having come into accord with the nature of all things. *Everything and everyone is going to die. Even my children are going to die.*

Although this may sound depressing and negative, I did not feel that way. Instead there was a clarity and sense of purpose to my life that seemed to have previously been missing.

The world is out of balance, I thought. It seemed to me, at the time, that most people spent their lives lost in a senseless state of craving—blindly running after material things and clinging to empty dreams. And I, too, had spent far too many hours caught up in the madness. I wanted to shout to the world, "Slow down! Wake up! Don't you know what's waiting for you at the end of the road you're frantically running down? Your coffin!" *Humans really haven't looked into their own impermanence,* I thought. *Most have not yet realized they are going to die.*

The story of the Buddha's first trip outside the palace walls came to mind. As a child, Siddhartha Gautama, the Buddha, was protected by his father, the king of the Shakya clan, so that he would never have to set his eyes on sadness or misery. Siddhartha was kept within the palace walls in luxurious surroundings. One day at the age of twenty-nine he ordered his servant to take him out of the palace so that he might see the world. And see the world he did. It is said that for the first time in his life, Siddhartha saw a man who was very old. He asked his servant, "What manner of being is this? His head is white and his body is withered and he can barely support himself on his staff."

He was told, "These are the symptoms of old age: this same man was once a youth; now, as years have passed, his beauty is gone and his body is wasting. All beings, sire, are subject to old age." Siddhartha was greatly affected by these words. "What joy or pleasure can people take," he thought, "when they know their body must soon wither?"

The next time they ventured out, Siddhartha saw someone sitting in a corner, shaking and calling out in pain, his body covered with boils. Again he asked his servant, "What manner of being is this? Why is he suffering so?" And again he was told that "all beings, the poor and the rich, the ignorant and the wise, all beings will one day know the pain of illness, just as this man." Siddhartha was deeply moved. All pleasures appeared stale to him, and he could take no joy in his life.

They ventured out a third time. On this occasion, Siddhartha came across a funeral procession. The young prince, shuddering at the sight of the lifeless body, asked, "What manner of being is this, and why are the others who follow him so grief stricken?" His servant replied, "This is a dead person, sire, a corpse. The life has left him, the light of his eyes is faded, his thoughts are still, and he will live no more. Those lamenting are his loved ones, carrying the body to the funeral pyre."

Astounded, the young Siddhartha asked if there were other instances of this in the world or if this was the only dead person. His servant told him that it was the same all over the world and that no one could escape old age, sickness, and death.

The prince's mouth opened in horror. "O worldly beings!" he gasped, "how fatal is your delusion! Inevitably your own bodies will crumble to dust, yet unheeding and carelessly, ye live on."

That Tuesday evening, I had become quite aware of the ills of existence, but by no means was I free of a sense of ego and attachment to this life.[10] "If it is true gold," I had heard my teacher say, "test it in fire." Spiritual insight must be tested in the fire of our everyday life. It is one thing to sit quietly and undisturbed in spiritual retreats, experiencing peace and happiness; it is quite another to take this practice into the world in order to reify it in the midst of activity.

Now was the time for me to redouble my efforts to focus on my spiritual practice. I knew that if I let my mind relax or run wild, it would lead me into darkness, despair, and self-pity. I could not let this happen. I told myself that practice was going to be different for a while, but never before in my life had it been more important for me to stay focused.

If only I could sit, do some formal Zen meditation, I thought. I tilted the bed up to do zazen as best I could and focused on my breath. Time passed while I sat absorbed in deep, silent breathing. I can do this! I thought. Whether I live or die, I must not lose sight of my true Mind. Now is my chance to test it in fire.

"Feelings, sensations, perceptions, and the formations of consciousness are all empty and transitory," I said. "Where will you take refuge through these most difficult times? In the body now weak and failing? In thoughts and mind states that cannot be grasped for even a moment?" I vowed to try to stay centered and not identify with or become attached to ephemeral states of mind. "Storms may come and go," I thought, "but the sky remains undisturbed."

I placed my hands together and repeated three times the Buddhist formula for taking refuge.[11]

I take refuge in Buddha.
I take refuge in Dharma.
I take refuge in Sangha.

Feeling tired and weak, I faded off to sleep as the realization of all I had been told began to sink in.

2

FACING DEATH

My body is given up,
Cast away.
Zero.
But on snowy nights
I feel chilly.

—JAPANESE WAKA POEM

Wednesday, August 30

THE NEXT MORNING I seemed to have found a measure of confidence to face the day with courage and determination. The previous night's reflection had reminded me of the necessity to focus on each and every moment. That afternoon my mom and I shared a few minutes alone while the rest of the family ate lunch. I told her how grateful I was for my fifteen years of Zen practice and that it was now preparing me for what was to come. Years ago many in my family, including my mother, had been bitterly disappointed when I abandoned Catholicism. Now, though, my mom was more comfortable with my Buddhist beliefs. Actually, I had not so much rejected Catholicism as I had been inexorably drawn to the Zen Buddhist path by my burning need to discover who and what I was.

I looked out the window and saw some large white clouds moving softly across a deep blue sky. "Mom," I said, "there is a Zen verse that says,

> Hundreds of flowers in spring, the moon in autumn,
> A cool breeze in summer, and snow in winter.
> If your mind is not clouded with unnecessary things,
> No season is too much for you.

"I hope to keep this 'no season is too much for you' state of mind throughout this ordeal. If I get off track, please keep reminding me." She promised that she would.

Thursday, August 31

The next afternoon I began to feel extremely tired. Along with the chemotherapy, I was also being given blood and platelets. I was short of breath and weaker than I had been since my admission. My temperature was rising fast and I began to experience rigors— convulsive, tremor-like spasms—caused by my body's reaction to the platelets. At times the rigors became so bad that it seemed as if I were going to jump right out of my bed. I began shivering uncontrollably, feeling chilled to the point of freezing. Then, within moments, I would relax and begin sweating profusely. Margaret began putting cold cloths on my head and chest. Then the rigors would begin again, and off would come the cold cloths and on would go the blankets. My family and I later referred to these nights as the "socks on, socks off" nights. Several times an hour I swung from chills and shivering, with requests for blankets and extra socks, to sweating and pleas for cold cloths and ice water.

Soon I was passing out and coming to, only to see my siblings placing cloths over my body. They had agreed to take shifts so that I would not be alone. That night it was Shirley-Anne and my brother Eric's turn. Each time I came to, I was greeted by warm smiles and looks of concern. It seemed as if I had known them forever. We were far too familiar with each other for them to even attempt to hide their fear and worry. Eric and Shirley-Anne had been practicing Zen for many years and we had been at several retreats together. Earlier that evening they had joined me in a chanting service. My weak chanting and nodding head were signs to us all that things were getting worse quickly.

"How are you feeling?" they asked. I smiled. Only moments before when the chills and rigors had become increasingly violent, they had climbed into my bed and hugged me tightly between them. With tears running down her cheeks, Shirley-Anne had looked at Eric and said, "I'm afraid we're going to lose him." All their attempts to warm the shivering, semiconscious body they held were unsuccessful. When I came to, I could see by the looks on their faces that they knew more about the seriousness of my condition than I did.

What they did not know was how much resolve I had in my heart. When Sensei had come to see me the day before, I expressed to her how comfortable I was with the thought of my dying. I had been experiencing great peace and a sense of lightness from having "let go," and I felt a tremendous freedom from coming to terms with the inevitability of my death. Thinking this to be a good thing, I told her that I was ready to go and was no longer afraid.

When she heard this, Sensei gave me a penetrating and concerned look. She then shared with me an experience she had had years before when she had "died" from an allergic reaction to a drug she had been given. She told me of the utter peace, the inexpressible wonder and beauty of that moment, and warned me that if given a choice whether to die or to come back, "You'll choose death. It's just too wondrous and too easy," she said. "Jim, if it hadn't been for my two daughters and my husband, I'm sure I would not be here today. It was because of their needs that I decided to come back; it was not because it was something I wanted to do. And even though you may not understand this, in that state of freedom and ease, it wasn't even all that important to me that my daughters were going to have to live without a mother and my husband without a wife. It's hard to explain this, Jim, but please do listen carefully."

She leaned close to me and in a loud whisper exclaimed, "Your family needs you! The *sangha* needs you! I need you! You must promise me that you will fight, and when and if the time comes to choose, *you will choose life.* Your work here is not over yet!"

At first I had been surprised that she was asking this of me. It would have been far easier just to let go, but her conviction that it was not yet my time to leave had made a deep impression on me and made me reconsider my accord with death. I gave her my word. Even so, I did not realize at that moment how deep this commitment went.

Through the days that followed, this resolve was always with me. Now, as I lay there with my brother and sister looking down at me, I knew that they too needed reassurance that I was going to give it my best shot. I thought of a story told by Roshi Kapleau on the last night of my first seven-day retreat. I was an unseasoned participant, and the talk that night made a great difference in my ability to carry on after sitting in meditation for long, tiring periods during the previous six days.

"I have a story for you," I whispered. Both my brother and sister looked at me, astonished that I was even moving my lips. I smiled and continued, "One night during the American Revolution, an American ship was taken by surprise by a British ship and took several hits before she could ready herself. The deck was in flames and many lives were lost. The British knew they had the upper hand and called out that the Americans must surrender immediately. If they did, all aboard would be spared. The captain sent back this message: *We have not yet begun to fight!* That ship went on to win the battle and many more that followed."

"You should know," I said, "that *I have not yet begun to fight.*"

Tears rolled down their faces. I returned a smile and a few tears of my own. They had never seen me so helpless, nor had they ever been in a situation where they felt so helpless. They had both trained with me for years in the martial arts. Here lay the person who had been their instructor for all that time, the person whose techniques and physical strength they had idealized. But tonight there was no doubt in any of our minds: I didn't even have the strength to urinate.

My spirit, though, was strong, and as I knew I could be very close to death, I asked my brother to read to me one of my favorite Buddhist texts. I pointed to the *Diamond Sutra;*[1] its succinct and straightforward teaching had always helped me focus my mind. "Please begin with chapter ten," I requested. My brother's voice seemed to penetrate my weakening body-mind:

> All bodhisattvas, lesser and great, should develop a pure,
>   lucid mind
> not depending on sound, flavor, touch, odor, or any
>   quality.
> A bodhisattva should develop a mind that alights upon
>   nothing whatsoever:
> and so should it be established.

I have no doubt that had I not entered those next few weeks with such a strong spirit and determination I would not be here today. I am so grateful that Sunyana-sensei was firm with me about choosing life and not giving up. I also know that if I hadn't been seasoned in the discipline of Zen training, I would have faced this whole crisis quite differently. The practice of returning again and again to the work at hand—regardless of enticements from the stubborn ego to do otherwise—has helped me develop the tenacity to keep moving forward during the most difficult times.

As Eric read to me, I felt grateful for the cold cloths Shirley-Anne was administering. Eric later told me how remarkable it was that after an hour or so of the rigors and extreme temperatures I would come to and repeat the last line I had heard from the *Diamond Sutra* as a signal for him to continue. Then, within moments, I would be gone again. This went on for hours. My brother and sister were tired and distressed by my deterioration. The rigors were now so extreme that I was shaking violently. No number of blankets seemed to help. I opened my eyes and saw their tired, worried faces. "Please get some rest," I said. "We're not leaving!" was their reply. I did not have the strength to argue.

With tears streaming down her face, Shirley-Anne told my mother in the morning, "I couldn't believe it. Here he was almost dead, without the strength even to sit up, and he was giving us an encouragement talk and urging us to get some rest. Mom, he just has to pull through. If anyone can, he can." They were hugging and crying when the alarm went off.

I had been having a difficult time breathing; it seemed to take all the energy I had just to inhale. I noticed my sister's eyes widen and her face become concerned, then I passed out. I had developed tachycardia, a dangerously rapid heartbeat. I was not receiving adequate oxygen in the brain and my heart rate increased dramatically to compensate. Shirley-Anne had been eyeing the heart monitor and noticed that my heartbeats jumped from 72 to 226 per minute. Then the alarm sounded. The nurses responded immediately, paged the doctors, and began administering oxygen.

A team of doctors brought the crash cart to my room, a cart with emergency equipment for resuscitating patients. My family noticed the paddles on the defibrillator, a machine that gathers electric charge in capacitors and then discharges it in a fraction of a second to help the heart resume its normal rhythm. My sister backed up to the wall. My brother and mother were on the verge of panic. A doctor calmly turned to my family and suggested that it might be best for them to wait in the hall. They were also told to summon Margaret immediately. My family was expecting to hear the inevitable "Clear" command. It didn't come—the defibrillator was never used.

When I revived, I was sitting up and several doctors were tapping on my back. The dead sound told them my lungs were filling with fluids. "You have double pneumonia, Mr. Bedard. Do you understand?" I understood, but I couldn't figure out what they wanted me to do about it. The weakness of my body was such that I could scarcely lift my head. With a feeble look I shrugged my shoulders as if to say, "What can I do? Please *do* something." I just wanted to get some rest and passed out.

Several times over the next year or so I would sense what felt to me like a sudden shift of responsibility: the doctors would imply that the responsibility for my welfare was in my own hands. It seemed that whenever we were about to enter into a new phase of treatment, I would meet with a group of doctors and we would discuss the team effort that would be required for us to succeed. But when the chips were down and I was in trouble, I often felt alone. It was at just those times that my family and I would be told, "It's up to him now." While it seemed to me at the time that I was being handed a huge burden, it was just the simple truth, an acknowledgment of the facts, modern medicine realizing its limitations.

Now, unconscious as I was, I received an urgent message to breathe, but I was too weak. I struggled to open my eyes, looking for someone to help me. It seemed that there were twenty people around me saying, "Breathe, Jimmy, keep breathing. You have to keep breathing." Someone placed a large orange ball in my hand and told me to squeeze it and not to stop. It was the portable oxygen kit. They were moving me to the intensive care unit, the ICU, fast. I remember dropping the rubber ball. Squeezing it made me feel better, but I didn't have the strength to keep it up. I felt completely helpless. Looking up at the nurse, with palms turned upward I shrugged as if to say, "I'm sorry. I can't."

I thought I was dying and tears came to my eyes. There was no room on the elevator for my wife, and I couldn't understand why, in these last moments of my life, I was surrounded by people I didn't know.

It was Friday morning, and Ian, Ross, and Randy were down the hall chanting, helping in the best way they could.

The doctors were very concerned. I had developed a systemic infection and they weren't sure what it was. I was taken to the operating room and a lung biopsy was taken through the mouth. The lungs were flushed to clear them of fluid and infections. I was taken to a private room in ICU and put on oxygen. My immune system was very low and they were afraid I might pick up other infections. Even with the oxygen it took an enormous effort just to breathe, and I was tiring quickly. Since this was causing too much stress for my heart, the doctors decided to hook me up to a respirator. When I came to again I couldn't breathe at all. I couldn't understand why some people were holding me down and others were choking me. *I can't breathe! Don't they know—I can't breathe!*

Even though I was too weak to lift my arms off the bed, I made an attempt to save myself. A few times in my life I had tapped into reserves of incredible energy and power when training in the martial arts. Delirious and confused, and not knowing who these people were, I sat up, pushed a nurse out of the way, and fought for my life. It was a dangerous thing to do, as the respirator was partially inserted, and because of my low platelets, any movement could have caused fatal internal bleeding. The doctor in charge ordered me sedated. I struggled to communicate to them. *They don't understand . . . I can't breathe!*

Somehow I became aware that these were doctors and nurses trying to help me. They too saw that something was terribly wrong. The respirator was not getting the oxygen to me. One nurse was urging me to relax. I did so for several seconds that seemed to last a lifetime. Nothing. The sedation was beginning to work. I had but seconds to let them know I still couldn't breathe, the tube was blocked, the machine was faulty, something was not working. I could tell they too were becoming anxious and concerned. In a last attempt to let them know that whatever it was they were trying wasn't working, I turned onto my side and kicked the fan off a small table by my bedside. My upper torso was now being held down by several people and I had the use of only this one leg. Having trained for more than fifteen years in the martial arts and having done thousands of kicks and self-defense techniques, it was this one weak, sloppy kick that saved my life.

A young nurse leaned over, inches from my face, asking, "What is it?" Her eyes widened when she saw the reason for the complication. My jaw was locked in a spasm, and I was biting the hose from the respirator. The hose was indeed blocked. The nurse grabbed my head firmly and, with her thumbs on either side, pried my jaws open. She urged me to relax my jaw. I focused on that area with whatever willpower I had left, and my jaw relaxed. A loud sound filled my ears as oxygen entered my lungs. I knew we had found the problem. Everyone in the room seemed to relax, and I slipped into darkness.

Back in the room I had come from, my empty bed was surrounded by my siblings and parents. My brother John returned from a break to find the family crying. John was never one to give up hope easily. He went to work at once offering encouragement and reassurance.

The doctors kept me sedated in ICU to prevent further bleeding in the lungs. My kidneys were failing, and the doctors searched without success for an antibiotic that would arrest the spreading infection. Not a drop of the nine and a half liters of fluids with different antibiotics that should have been passing through my kidneys was being voided. My cheeks were so swollen that my nose seemed to disappear. My blood pressure was completely out of line, and liver function tests indicated serious problems.

That night it was my youngest sister, Cindy-Lee, and John's turn to stay with me. They worked through the night bathing me in cold cloths. The fever was increasing and they could not keep my body cool.

Saturday, September 2

The next morning a nurse told my mother, "You know, I have been working in intensive care for almost twenty years, and I have never seen anything like what I have witnessed these past few nights. Your children have not left Jim's side for even a moment. You can just see the love in their faces as they tend to him. Mrs. Bedard, you have a very special family."

Later that day the ICU doctor explained to Margaret that all the tests were coming back negative and they were unable to identify the bacteria. "None of the antibiotics seem to be helping. Jim is in very critical condition."

"How serious is it?" asked Margaret. "Our daughter is here, but the boys are still at home. Should I have them come in?"

"This will be very scary for the children, Mrs. Bedard, but as far as Jim's condition is concerned, I think he has about three hours left." Margaret's immediate thought was, *Those poor children, to have to live without their father.*

"I want to call them in to see Jim," she said. "They would want to be here."

Our friend and neighbor Jill picked up the boys in Bethany and began the long drive to Toronto.

Margaret notified the family, and my siblings and their spouses each took a turn spending time alone in my small room saying good-bye. It was a wrenching time for everyone. Shirley-Anne later said how unreal the possibility of my death seemed. "It was even more difficult," she told me, "because the guy on the bed didn't look anything like my brother."

Not only was my body swollen from excess fluids, but my skin was yellow from infections and liver problems, and my hands and feet were blue from lack of oxygen in the blood. A feed tube ran through my nose to my stomach for suctioning. A catheter was inserted for urinating. There were seven other tubes coming into my body to administer antibiotics, blood products, platelets, and chemotherapy drugs. I was under sedation so that I would not move and cause hemorrhaging in my lungs.

Meanwhile, Margaret was praying that the children would arrive in time to find their father alive and be able to say their good-byes. When Jason, Bradley, and Raymond arrived at the hospital, they were greeted by my father and their uncles, who were in tears. Bradley said it was the first time he had ever seen his grandparents crying. His aunts hugged him and also broke into tears. Margaret met with the children to tell them about the gravity of my condition. Even before she had a chance to tell them, they suspected the worst. Amanda had overheard Eric tell his wife that the doctors thought I had no more than a few hours left.

There was a limit of two people at a time allowed into my small ICU room. Margaret asked, "Who wants to go in first?" Amanda had already seen me, so it was up to the boys to decide. The two older ones looked at each other and agreed that they were not yet up to it, that they wanted a few minutes to collect themselves. Raymond spoke up, "I'll go in Mom," he said, "but I want you to come with me."

Ray's first words were, "Wow! What happened to him Mom? I've never seen Dad so fat before." Margaret told him about the kidney failure and fluid retention. Ray said, "Can you hear me Dad? I love you Dad. Keep fighting Dad. I know you can do it." I was trying to open my eyes, trying to say something. I wanted to respond. The most important thing for me was to make this as easy as possible for our children, but I was unable to communicate. Margaret noticed that I was trying to open my eyes to no avail. After a while they said their good-byes and left.

Once outside the ICU, Raymond said to Margaret, "I feel so sorry for you, Mom, cause now you're gonna have to be the mom and the dad." The other children took turns visiting and saying good-bye.

As soon as they met the others in the waiting room, Margaret said, "He'll make it, I know he will. He'll do it for his children.

They have always been his strength." She then sat down, tired and confused, trying to believe what she was saying. The rest of the family were concerned that she might be in denial and not preparing herself for the inevitable.

For the next few hours it was touch and go. A team of ICU doctors met with my hematologist and the specialist from infectious diseases. They were baffled that none of the antibiotics was helping. My hematologist pointed out that my blood counts were so low that even with the help of antibiotics there was only a very slight chance for recovery. They agreed to try a very powerful antibiotic as a last attempt to get ahead of the infections. My liver was failing and my spleen had shut down. This next move might be fatal, but without it, there would be no chance of survival. Margaret was consulted and told how seriously this new drug would affect my kidneys, which were already failing.

"We may have to put him on kidney dialysis," the doctors told her, "and that would be risky. The surgeons feel that because his platelets are so low, there is a strong chance he could bleed to death." Nevertheless, they felt this treatment might be necessary to remove unwanted waste from my blood that made it more difficult for my body to deal with infections. They were also considering operating. They had not been successful in identifying the infection with the first lung biopsy, and they hoped to cut through the ribs to get a better sample for testing. But my hematologist and the surgeon cautioned the infectious-disease specialists against it. With my platelets so low this procedure also would be impossible.

Margaret was confused; she was in such anguish that it was impossible for her to make serious medical decisions. She did not feel qualified; she couldn't even decide what to eat or feed the children. "Do what you think is best," she finally replied.

Shirley-Anne came to see me and found that my hands had turned a darker blue and were icy cold. She left the room alarmed and told the others that she felt they were losing me. Mike, however, had noticed that my chest was still warm and that my face color had actually improved. He urged everyone to stay positive and not give up hope. He later told me that after he convinced the rest of the family, he prayed for the faith to believe that what he was saying was true.

Sunyana-sensei was in Toronto that day, a week after my first night in the hospital. She was leading a workshop at our center, a full-day introduction to Zen practice that included talks, question periods, and instruction in meditation. During every break, Sensei came to the hospital to be at my bedside. At one point she and my mother came in together to see me—my mother a longtime devout Catholic, with her rosary in hand, and my Zen teacher a Buddhist priest, with her *juzu* beads.[2]

My mother looked at Sunyana-sensei and said, "I don't know much about Zen Buddhism, but I believe we can heal him, or at least help him a great deal if we pray over him." Sensei said, "Yes, we can." So an interesting chanting service began. On one side of my bed the rosary was being recited with a mother's love and a hopeful heart. On the other side, my Buddhist teacher chanted the *Kannon Sutra*[3] single-mindedly. My mother wrote in her journal that night:

> It was wonderful to see that even though the chanting and prayers seemed different to the ears, the love and affection for this one man who lay there helpless united our traditions and transcended all differences. I knew in my heart that he had no choice but to get better.

When I did come to, several days later, this was one of the first things I heard about. Even though I barely had the strength to speak, I asked my mother to get Sensei on the phone. I greeted her with "Wow, that was a close one!" There was silence on the other end; she was in tears and so was I. After a few moments I told her that my mother had just told me about that interesting chanting service in ICU. Then, in a weak voice, I continued, "Don't you know how dangerous that was?"

"Dangerous?" came the reply.

With my mother listening at my bedside, I explained, "Not dangerous for me, but for you two."

There was more silence, but I could picture a smile on my teacher's face not unlike the one that was creeping across my mother's face.

"Now," I said, "just imagine if only *one half* of me were to get healed, one of you and your faith would be in a lot of trouble."

We laughed and shed a few tears.

"Well, Jim, you certainly haven't lost your sense of humor," remarked Sunyana-sensei.

"No, that's true," I replied. "That will be the last thing to go."

But for now there was no laughter in my room and no humor in the waiting room. Things were not going well and the doctors suspected that it was still only a matter of hours before I would be gone. My wife, children, and family took shifts sitting quietly by my bed, all day and on through the night.

Sunday, September 3

The next day I was even closer to death than before. My Zen teacher visited again. This time Margaret wanted to meet with her first. Although Margaret does not practice Zen, she was somewhat familiar with Zen Buddhist practices and knew that death was considered an important transition period. She had heard me tell of times when a Zen priest or other experienced practitioner had helped a dying person in the last hours. Margaret wanted reassurance that Sunyana-sensei was not going to help me prepare for death. "You must promise me that you won't even mention it, not till the very end," Margaret insisted. Sensei reassured her that she definitely would not do so unless the whole family asked her to, and then she entered my small isolation room.

It was the only time I would surface to consciousness for days. I opened my eyes to find this Kannon-like figure standing in formal Buddhist attire at my bedside. There was no doubt in my mind that she had been chanting. It can sometimes take years, even lifetimes, for one to begin to understand the karmic relationship one has with a spiritual teacher. For me that day, in that one look I realized more about how I came to meet her, our past relationships, and the significance of her being there at that time, than I ever could have learned from hearing or reading about it. Tears of gratitude ran down my face and filled my ears.

I am convinced to this day that she called me back. I was dying and I knew it. More than anything else I wanted to communicate to her what I had just experienced. Unable to identify with my body, I had become acutely aware of other realms of existence. This so confirmed my faith in the dharma and in Sensei's teachings that I wanted to notify her so she could tell others of my confirmation journey, but I was too weak. It was not until months later that I could talk about what I had experienced that day.

At about this time, Roshi Kapleau found a picture of me taken a year earlier when I had visited him in Florida. He enlarged it so that it could be used during chanting services to help people focus their energy and attention on me. Roshi knew well how effective such services are in helping others regardless of the distance between them and the chanters. "Our fundamental Mind is not limited by time or space," he often said.

Roshi sent this picture to Zen centers in Rochester, Toronto, Vermont, and other places. On this critical day and many others, chanting services were held for me in Poland, Sweden, Costa Rica, and several cities in Canada and the United States. My mother and my sister Cindy-Lee did some networking of their own and had masses said on my behalf in churches around the country. It is no small thing to have so many people focused on the welfare of one individual. I will be forever grateful for the help I received in those desperate times, and I know now, in my heart, that when I chant for the benefit of all sentient beings, I am helping in a very real way.

That evening, when Eric was visiting, he felt I was trying to communicate with him. I kept tapping my chest with my fingers and making a motion as if I were trying to pull something out. This disturbed him to no end, as he knew I was asking for help. He was very tired and left to return to the hotel to get some rest. At six sharp on Monday morning he awoke and felt he had the answer. "Jim wants to be set free!" he exclaimed. He told Margaret that he felt I was aware that I was on life support and that I knew I was dying and wanted to let go. Margaret rushed to the hospital immediately and demanded a meeting with the ICU doctors.

Her question was direct: "Is Jim on life support? Because I don't think he would want that."

The doctor took Margaret's hand, looked her in the eye, and replied, "Mrs. Bedard, Jim still has a fighting chance. His heart is strong and his mind is fine. This is just a stepping stone to health if we can help him pull through." He continued, "Sure, if you want to get technical, your husband is on life support. So is everyone who has an operation or is given antibiotics. I think we should give him a chance to see if he can pull through this."

It was just what Margaret wanted to hear.

Again they came in to visit me, and again I was motioning for the removal of something. But this time it was different. I was wincing from pain, and the doctor noticed that my hand was directly over my gallbladder.

"I think your husband has gallstones, Mrs. Bedard. We will order an ultrasound immediately. And when you are in seeing him, it might be good to tell him that he is not on life support."

More complications, more to worry about. *Surely they won't be able to do a gallbladder operation, my family were thinking. Just yesterday the doctors* were saying that his counts were too low for him to be put on dialysis or to have the lung biopsy through the ribs.

The ultrasound doctor came in with a portable machine. There was no indication of gallstones. Other complications were evident with the spleen and the pancreas, both of which showed signs of swelling and malfunctioning. The doctor told Margaret and the rest of my family that because the liver and the spleen were enlarged, I was experiencing a great deal of pain. It was crucial for the new antibiotic to kick in before the chemo began to work and the platelet and red cell counts began to drop. "Keep your fingers crossed," the doctors said. "We still have a few days before things start to crash."

My family all took turns trying to convince me that I was not on life support. The doctor who told them to do this must have had experience with patients who have come out of deep comas or long periods of being unconscious. I don't know how I heard, but I do remember different members of my family telling me that I was not on life support. Since this wasn't an issue for me at the time, I couldn't understand why they kept repeating it. At one point Michael told me that there were no blast cells found in the blood samples taken that day and that this could be an indication that the leukemia was in remission. Even though I seemed completely unconscious, when I heard the news I placed my hands palm-to-palm over my heart, and was gone again.

From this experience I learned something of great importance: hearing is a direct channel to our innermost consciousness. If I ever visit someone who seems to be "not with us," I will remember this lesson. What is said in the room and to that person is essential. I'm sure we can comfort people and help guide them at their time of death in ways that cannot be measured or explained.

The next few days continued to be stressful for my wife, children, family, and friends. There were times the doctors thought my condition was stabilizing, and then, shortly after, the family would again be told to say their good-byes.

At one point when things were looking particularly grim, Amanda became discouraged and depressed. Mike took her aside and told her about my telling the "I have not yet begun to fight" story. "Never give up on your father, Amanda. He has a strong spirit." She then went to the chapel with Cindy-Lee and her husband, Brian, and said the rosary.

Visiting in ICU was now limited to family only. Ross, Ian, and Randy were not permitted to come in and see me. They knew I would have wished to have the Prajña Paramita chanted at my bedside in my last moments, but they did not want to be assertive in any way that might cause stress and complicate matters further. Instead, they chanted in the waiting room. When I heard of this later, I insisted that these friends were to have the same access to my bedside as my immediate family. Indeed, for me they were family.

My condition began to stabilize, and the doctor said that they expected things would continue to improve until the onset of the effects of the chemotherapy drugs. "Then," he said, "we will just have to wait and see."

On Tuesday afternoon my son Brad, the athlete of the family, and my brother-in-law Brian came in to visit. Brad and I had often jogged together, and he had gotten used to being able to beat me to the house on the last lap. This night he was feeling very confused and angry. It really didn't seem fair; his father was quite healthy just a few weeks ago.

"Can you hear us, Jim?" Brian said. "Brad's here. Say hello to your father, Brad." I heard a weak, "Hi, Dad. Just don't give up, okay, Dad?" I struggled to open my eyes and managed to do so just as they were about to leave. Brad looked very frightened and Brian had a sweet smile on his face. Managing a weak smile of my own, without raising my arm off the bed, I gave Brad the thumbs up with my right hand. I only wished I could have conveyed my thoughts: Don't worry, pal, this fight's not over yet!

I then looked down at my feet—they were very swollen and

blue. I remember passing out puzzled, wondering *What have they done to my feet?* I had never seen them so big or so blue.

When the rest of the family heard that I had given Brad the thumbs up, there were cheers and a lot of hugging in the waiting room. My family and friends locked each other in a group embrace trying to build up their hopes. All were working hard to stay positive. When emotions ebbed and tears were plentiful, John would call the family together and give them a pep talk. "Have some faith," he would say. "If we mourn him now, then we've given up on him. We have to stay positive. He can do this with our help." Then he would find an empty room, place his hands over his face, and cry, trying to believe his own encouragement talks.

My father and some of my siblings and their spouses decided to return home. They had been away from business and children for several days and had things to attend to, but their leave was short. Once home they found it too difficult to be so far away given my lack of improvement and unstable condition. The next day they returned. It was Wednesday, only ten days after my having been diagnosed with acute myeloid leukemia.

3

STARTING OVER

Without undergoing a winter
that bites into your bones
How can the plum blossoms regale you
with their piercing fragrance?

—HUANG PO

A FEW DAYS LATER, still in ICU, I came to and was startled to
see a stranger's face staring directly into my eyes. It seemed quite
large because it was so close. I was greeted by smiling eyes above
a hygiene mask and a look of expectation, but only returned a
questioning, puzzled look. With this, the face became very concerned and pulled away, looking toward the nurse. The nurse got
up and came over to my bed.

"Jim, you remember Margaret, don't you? You know, Margaret
. . . your wife."

I looked into Margaret's anxious eyes. I was wondering, *What
the hell is going on? I don't know who these people are or where I am.*

Margaret just kept smiling at me, but I could tell she was becoming uneasy.

"Do you know what year it is Jim?" the nurse asked. The first
year that came to mind was 1963, but somehow I knew that

wasn't right. With the respirator hooked up, I couldn't have spoken anyway, but I didn't even nod in acknowledgment. The nurse asked Margaret to remove her mask so I could get a better look at her. She did, and again showed me a smiling, hopeful face. Feeling very ill and tired, I wanted to rest and was gone again.

The masks were for my protection. I was in no condition to fight another virus. Intermittently over the next year I would spend four or five months in isolation, and at those times I became quite familiar with the protocol for visitors: strict hand washing before entering my room, no physical contact, and at certain times, visitors in masks. In consequence, I often felt distant from people at a time when hugs and intimacy were what I needed most, but I had suffered a great deal and knew that it was very important for me not to pick up another infection. I remember once sitting up in bed, looking at my eleven-year-old son standing in the doorway blowing kisses to me. He had a cold and the medical staff didn't want him in my room. I wished I could hug him, but I had to play it safe and keep my distance. If I survived, there would be plenty of time for hugs later. When it came to choosing between feeling uncomfortable and feeling safe, I chose the latter.

The next visit from Margaret was better—well, at least I remembered I was married. Within a few minutes of talking, a floodgate in my mind seemed to open and waves of old memories poured in. I was confused and knew I was not doing well. There was a great deal of pressure in my chest, and I was no longer in charge of my body. Even my breathing was being controlled by an outside force.

It was clear to everyone that I wanted the respirator out. That night Margaret met with the doctor on call. He came in to see me and was very specific. He told me that he was prepared to take out the respirator as long as I agreed to let him put it back in again if it became necessary. I agreed. What he did not tell me was that my blood pressure was very high and he suspected that my irritation with the respirator exacerbated the problem. Unfortunately that was not the case. After the respirator was removed, my blood pressure did not come down, and, as I was still sedated, Margaret and my mother had to spend the night waking me and reminding me to breathe. I couldn't believe my ears.

"Breathe, Jimmy, keep breathing, Jimmy. Jimmy! Jimmy! You have to keep breathing honey . . . keep breathing. . . ." It seemed to be a continuation of what had just happened on the elevator on my way to ICU, but that had taken place a week earlier.

My goodness, I thought, have I forgotten how to breathe? Shouldn't that just happen automatically? I must be in really bad shape.

The next time I awoke I saw what I thought were two nurses in street clothing standing looking over me. "Hi! How are you feeling?" they said. Again I responded with a quizzical look. They turned toward each other with sad, forced smiles.

"I don't think he knows us," one of them was saying to the other.

"Hey! It's me, your sister, Shirley-Anne." "Hi Jim. It's me, Cindy-Lee."

"You remember Cindy-Lee and me, we're your sisters." They both lifted up their masks to show me their faces. Though they seemed familiar I could not remember where I had seen them before.

When my two sisters came to visit me again, I recognized them and asked how and where they had changed their clothes. They told me that they had been home for a few days to look after their children and had just returned to the hospital. Minutes later I turned to Cindy-Lee and asked, "When did you get here?" I had just been talking to her moments before. She was unsettled but, like everyone else in the family, had become a master at disguising her fear and worry. She kept encouraging me to keep up the fight and get the rest I needed. Knowing I was lost in confusion, I surrendered to rest when I could and accepted my bewildered mind states almost as well as my family did.

The next day I awoke to the nurse in ICU turning on a radio for me. She felt that music would ease the monotony of the small, windowless room. It was a kind gesture, but the music made me feel nauseated. Each time I told her politely that the music was not to my liking she tried a new station. It didn't seem to matter what station she turned to, music was not the answer. Not yet anyway. Finally, I had to ask her to turn it off.

Because I had been motionless for so long, my senses had become very acute. It was as if I had no boundaries, no resistance. The music seemed to invade my body-mind. Sounds, and especially smells, pierced my defenses and made me feel uncomfortably vulnerable. Often I could tell what people had eaten for lunch as soon as they entered my room. I had to ask Mike, who smoked a pipe, not to bring it when he visited. I could smell it in his pocket even when he was more than ten feet away.

As I looked about, there seemed to be a hundred machines around me. I became aware of the many tubes coming to my body from intravenous bags and pumps. There was a tube through my nose for feeding me and suctioning out my stomach. An infrared light clamped to my toe read blood oxygen levels and a blood pressure monitor was fastened to my left arm. Every couple of minutes one of the pumps would beep and a nurse would come to adjust something, to change an IV bag, or to put a pill under my tongue.

One young nurse came in regularly. He had a great sense of humor and often made me laugh, but he always seemed to be a little confused and disoriented. My mother told me that she also felt he had a great bedside manner, but she was very nervous when it was his turn to hook up an intravenous bag or administer chemotherapy. He reminded me of comedian Don Knotts. One time he disconnected one of my lines and got so entangled in the other lines that he tripped and had to start over. I thought it quite comical, but my mother was so worried that he would hook up the wrong bag or insert a used needle into her son that she would not take her eyes off him.

The next time I awoke, Margaret was again at my bedside.

"How are the kids?" I asked.

"They're fine," replied Margaret, looking less frightened than the last time I had seen her. "They're in school, and they will be coming to Toronto to visit tomorrow night."

"In school? I thought school didn't start until the week after next." Now it was I who looked to the nurse, puzzled.

"You've been out for a long time, honey," Margaret said reassuringly. "There's lots to tell and your family is here waiting to see you, but for now you should just rest."

Ten days had passed, but for me it seemed to be just a matter of minutes. There were so many questions pressing upon me: Where was I? How were the kids doing with all of this? What were all these IV bags full of? Most important of all was the one burning question in my heart.

"Margaret," I asked, "did they have you call the family in?"

She hesitated. "No, but they've been here off and on to visit you." Her hesitation caused me to suspect that she might not be telling me the whole story.

"Is my mom here?" I asked.

"Yes, she's just outside the door. Would you like her to come in?"

"Sure. Let me talk to her alone for a moment. Would that be okay with you?" There was a suspicious look in her eyes, but she said it was fine and left.

My mother looked worried when she entered the room but happy to see me awake. After receiving a hug and a kiss on the forehead, I asked, "Mom . . . did they have you call in the family?" My mother knew this was my way of asking, "Am I dying?"

"No, honey, everyone is here because they love you and want to be with you."

I wasn't sure I was getting the straight goods. It was the truth, though. By the time I had come to, my condition was no longer critical. My family had been told by the doctors that it was important for me not to get discouraged, not to give up. It was essential that I keep fighting.

Nevertheless, my mind was on dying. Terminally ill or elderly people often wish for death, regarding it as the ultimate peace. If only this were the case. Nothing can be destroyed; life continues after death. There is life after life—death is only an important period of transition. After the dropping of the body, our next existence will be determined by our past actions and our state of mind at the time of our death. Therefore, it was important for me to die properly, with my mind at peace.

The oxygen mask I wore was like none I had seen before. It had a much larger hose than usual and on the mask itself there were three "horns" about five inches long extending from three holes in the mask. These intensified the oxygen levels by increasing the volume available and enabled me to stay off the respirator.

When Amanda came to visit, I said, "Look at how your father has regressed. I'm looking more and more like a dinosaur every day." It became known as the triceratops mask. If I took it off even for a moment, I would immediately become exhausted and my blood oxygen level would drop dramatically.

A nurse was assigned to my room full-time. He or she would either sit at the foot of my bed watching the monitors or, if I had visitors, sit in a chair outside my door. There were a few times when they would leave for short moments, and those were the times that my family were most nervous. One time when Margaret was alone with me, before I had been put on the triceratops mask, the hose to the respirator popped off and I exhaled—but there was no inhalation to follow. The alarm sounded and Margaret frantically forced the hose onto the tube and waited for what seemed like a very long time for the nurse to return. Within moments they had me hooked up properly. Margaret sank into her chair and stared wide-eyed at her husband, wondering if she would ever get a chance to tell him about it.

I was plagued by thirst—I cannot remember ever having been so thirsty. For more than a week I had neither eaten nor had a drink. I asked the nurse on call to please get me some water. She came in with a small Styrofoam cup. Since I could barely lift my arm off the bed, she helped me bring the cup to my mouth. To my great disappointment, there was no water in it, just two small slivers of ice. I relished them and asked for more. I was chagrined when the nurse gently but firmly told me that my ice chips were to be rationed for the next several days. I was not allowed food or fluids in case they had to resuscitate me or hook me up to the respirator again. Fluids in the stomach could cause vomiting. It was to be ice chips for now.

When my mom and Margaret were visiting again, I begged them to convince the nurses to increase the ice chip rations. I was so thirsty.

"There is one nurse on the night shift," I said, "who brings me half a cup of ice chips at a time. But the ones on day shift will only give me one or two chipped cubes. Please see if you can get them to give me a few more ice chips."

Because I was too weak to lift my head, I couldn't pour the cup without spilling it, so I would finger the chips to my mouth. That's how I figured out a way to cheat. Each time a nurse brought me half a cup or so of chips, I placed my fingers in the cup while savoring one of the chips, and the heat from my hand would help melt the others. Then I would have a small drink. It is impossible to describe how wonderful it was to have those few teaspoons of cold liquid. Several times I brought my hands together, with all the tubes in tow, and placing them over my heart in gassho, would feel deeply connected to the thousands of beings who must deal with thirst on a regular basis. I also thought often of the realm of thirsty spirits and hungry ghosts.[1] I now understood the suffering of hunger and thirst. I would never want to be reborn in that realm, I thought. One must be so careful. Then I prayed for all thirsty beings throughout the universe.

I spent the next few days and nights awake. Although I had great difficulty breathing and was extremely tired, I simply could not rest. There was no sight of the outdoors in the isolation room in ICU. A large window in the room faced the intensive care unit next to me and was covered for privacy. A smaller window in the door was viewless. Unable to move, I looked at the block wall at the foot of my bed and the large clock mounted there. I looked from side to side until the weak muscles of my neck grew tired and I would again spend my time watching the second hand make its way around the clock. I did not close my eyes in sleep for three days and three nights. Never has time passed so slowly or the minutes seemed so endless. Even though I was lying flat on my back with nothing to do, the experience was not at all restful. I longed for rest.

It felt miserable to have no control. My body was crying: Stop the poison and drink water. I could do neither. Water was denied despite my pleas. My system was being saturated with toxic drugs. I did not resist the drugs or put up a fight. I felt it was too late; it didn't matter anymore; I really didn't think I had long to live anyway. Rest was the only thing I really cared about, and this too seemed out of my reach.

A certain nurse who had a very compassionate and caring nature suggested that I take a sleeping pill to get some rest. "I really don't think I should take any more drugs," I replied. He looked around the room at the multitude of medications being administered to my body. Then he looked at me with eyebrows slightly raised as if to say, "Do you really think this little pill is going to make any difference?" But I had lost control of my life, and there were only these few small decisions that required my input. When your whole world has been reduced to such minor choices, they take on unimaginable proportions. I took no pill that night.

On the third sleepless night, I finally summoned that friendly nurse. He sat by my bed and, realizing my dilemma, patiently responded to my questions about the long-term effects of taking sleeping pills and possible addiction. He reassured me that my concerns were unfounded and that if I were ever to have a problem with sleep in the future because of having taken those pills in ICU, I should look him up personally.

"Jim," he said, "you haven't even begun to deal with what your body is going through, let alone the emotional work of dealing with having AML leukemia. Your rest is far more important than worrying about taking a few sleeping pills."

I agreed to take the pills. Even so, I lay awake for hours, and then requested more. It wasn't until the next afternoon that I actually slept for a few hours.

The effects of the chemotherapy were beginning, and I was too weak even to roll onto my side. My hemoglobin—the red blood cells that distribute oxygen throughout the body—was falling fast. The doctors told Margaret and my family that the infection was still not responding to antibiotics and that my spleen was not allowing the body to retain platelets. There was the ever present danger of internal bleeding. In addition, my blood pressure was very high despite medication to lower it. With high blood pressure and low platelets there was a strong likelihood of stroke or heart problems.

My liver was still swollen and painful. When the body is strong, it can mount a defense against intense pain, but I had no such reserves. I was limp and helpless. Waves of pain swept through me without resistance. Surprisingly, a sense of freedom came with this unintentional, reflexive acceptance of pain. There was no one standing against the pain. At times it was as though the pain, like drifting clouds, would appear and disappear without my involvement. My mind seemed lucid and clear.

I remembered my Zen teacher's admonitions about dealing with mental distractions that come when meditating. "Don't take hold of your thoughts—try to ignore them," she said. "Focusing on them, paying attention to them, repressing them, or becoming attached to them will only make them stronger. By returning to your practice, eventually persistent thoughts will leave."

Perhaps it was because I was so weak that there were so few intruding thoughts in my mind. I did not have the strength to pay attention to extraneous mental projections when I was in severe pain. I am convinced, though, that often the clarity came as a result of the chanting, meditation, and prayers that were said on my behalf. There were times, during a chanting service held by my dharma brothers and sisters or during a retreat that was going on when I was in the hospital, that tears of gratitude would run down my face and soak my gown even though I was racked by pain. Often when I spoke with Sunyana-sensei, I would mention how thankful I was to be experiencing this deep gratitude during the most difficult time of my life. At other times all I could feel was pain and suffering.

When I next came to, after my brief hours of sleep, my thirst was unbearable. I begged for a drink. I cried to my wife and mother, "Why can't I just have a little drink? Isn't it enough that I have to deal with this pain in my side and the headaches, the restless, sleepless nights and the nausea? Why do I have to experience this terrible thirst as well?"

When really thirsty, one comes to a point where having a drink is more important than anything else, and I needed a drink. The doctor on call was told about my change in spirits. Margaret said I was becoming agitated and discouraged. The nurse came into my room and asked if I could hold on for a while longer. She would see about getting me some Popsicles. When she got the okay from the doctor, we discovered that on that Sunday afternoon there were no Popsicles on our ward. Margaret and my mother checked the other floors without success. They told us we would have to wait for Monday's grocery delivery. I wasn't waiting.

I asked Margaret and my mother to check the ward to see if anyone else was also going without Popsicles. There were indeed several other patients who were wishing for these sweet flavored "ice-kabobs." The order was now clear—we needed to buy a few dozen. No one should have to suffer such thirst.

My first meal, drink, and dessert in more than ten days was an orange Popsicle. I was ten again. I could feel the wind in my hair as I sat on the porch of the local corner store, a young kid relishing his Popsicle. Orange had always been my favorite, and I was even more pleased because I was able to buy a round for the house.

What I didn't know was that with chemotherapy drugs I had lost a great deal of mucus membrane. Sores covered the roof of my mouth and ran all the way down the esophagus into the stomach. The cold wet fluid from the Popsicle made my stomach feel very upset. I experienced severe heartburn and some mild vomiting, but it was well worth it.

Most of the nurses knew my name, since they had been speaking to me for more than a week, but I was meeting them all for the first time. It was interesting for someone normally uncomfortable in anything but full attire to lie there without a stitch of clothing on and not feel naked. It was their body: they tended to its needs, bathed it, fed it, inserted tubes, removed tubes, and took blood from its arms, Hickman line, and other lines. They swabbed its throat, ears, groin, and rectum to check for bacteria. I had surrendered my most prized possession to a team of experts and was quite accepting of all the probes, pokes, and hot and cold sensations they assaulted me with.

I found myself indifferent when nurses male or female came into the room and bathed me, ran a hose up my nose to suction out the stomach, or wiped my buttocks and groin with an antibacterial soap so that I wouldn't pick up another infection. I never felt self-conscious or embarrassed. I was far too helpless.

The first day the catheter was removed, I asked my sisters, who were attending me that day, to hold the "blue jug" for me to urinate in. They were both very patient, but nothing came despite real signals from my body that it was a good idea to urinate. I looked up at my sisters and said in all sincerity, "I've forgotten how."

I was looking for help. But even if they had been of the same sex, there is no doubt in my mind that there was little they could have done. "I know you have to push somewhere," I said with a slight smile, "but I can't locate that spot." After a long wait I did manage to make a small contribution. Actually, I was more like a passive bystander experiencing that warm sensation again for the first time.

"It will come with practice, Mr. Bedard," the nurse reassured me. She then said, "The physiotherapist will be here soon. We'd like to get you started on an exercise program. We don't want muscle atrophy to cause long-term problems."

"You're not serious," I said. She was.

The physiotherapist had the same name as our dog and the same color hair. I don't know if she minded my telling her so, but we seemed to hit it off immediately. She asked me to lift my extended arms off the bed five times each side, then repeat the same with my legs. After an exhausting workout that lasted almost four minutes I was ready for a rest. "If you can do that once more today and again before I come back tomorrow, we will try to have you sit up in bed in the morning." The therapist seemed pleased with my efforts and left with a few words of encouragement.

When my mother rejoined Margaret and me, I proudly told her about my grueling exercise program and how well I had done. Only a few weeks before, I had been at the YMCA with Jason and Bradley and had worked out for a good half hour on the exercise bike, then spent an hour toying with the weights. I had always exercised regularly and was in pretty good shape before my illness. But there was a time several years earlier when I had been in *great* shape.

I had taught martial arts for more than ten years. Often I would run six miles before teaching two classes, then, after numerous sword cuts, kicks, punches, blocks, and many other exercises and techniques, I would go off to the gym with my brother Eric for an hour and a half on the weights.

One time a friend from the weight club came to visit my martial arts school. We were both competitive by nature. He often poked fun at me, calling me a scrawny wimp (I was 5 feet 11 inches tall and weighed 165 at the time), and I would tease him, telling him that he was carrying too much excess baggage. When he came to check us out, he bragged to the other students about how many push-ups he could do. He asked me what I thought my best was, and I told him I didn't know because I had never counted. "But," I added, "I'll do twenty-five more than you do right now."

With his hands shoulder width apart and palms flat, he did fifty push-ups. He did his best to hide his struggle on the last few, then stood proudly with his right hand turned up and said, "Well?" I dropped onto my knuckles and did a quick seventy-five push-ups without slowing at all, then moved to the front of the mat and began the workout with four hundred stride jumps. By the end of the class we had done a couple hundred more push-ups and many other exercises.

No doubt about it, I was showing off. Normally I would have just walked away from his challenge, but I felt he had great potential and I hoped to hook him in to our nonviolent style of training by impressing him with the qualities he respected: strength and endurance. Now I see the pride and ego from which these competitive attitudes stemmed, though he did join the club and in time became one of my better black belt students.

Eventually, I gave up the martial arts altogether. I no longer had any affinity with the techniques. Even after working with an aikido master to alter our training to teach self-defense techniques that did not involve actually striking someone, I had to surrender to my deepest inclinations. It was not for me. The better I became, the more pride I had to deal with. Besides, I simply could no longer bring myself to practice any martial art rooted in the duality of self versus other. I felt that the true spirit of the masters of the past was being lost, and that most of the focus had turned to comparing oneself with others and learning how to dominate them. Most practices stemmed from a need to defend the self. My Zen training confirmed again and again that there is no self to defend. "The best self-defense," I told my students in my last year there, "is good karma."

This illness was creating balance in my life. My exercise was now at the other end of the spectrum. Right arm up five times. Rest. Left arm up five times. Rest. My brother Michael was watching these pathetic movements. He had such a sorrowful look on his face that I could sense his concern and embarrassment for me. I said with a smile, "It's okay, Mike. It's good to be working out again."

Throughout this ordeal I never felt awkward about my looks or predicament. I tried with all my heart to just be, always returning to the question, Who am I at this moment? In one of the Buddhist sutras it is written that "past mind is unattainable, future mind is unattainable, and present mind is unattainable." Identifying strongly with our past gives it a greater hold on us. This can make change for the better more difficult. True, the present is imbued with the past, but no one can doubt the truth of past mind is unattainable. Future mind too, it is easy to understand, is "unattainable." But what about "present mind is unattainable"?

No matter where I looked for this present mind, it was nowhere to be found. States of mind would come and go, but there was nothing to grasp. Here I lay exhausted and suffering nausea and headaches, asking myself, *Who or what is aware of these transient formations of consciousness?* At times there was a sense of liberation and great freedom: *There is nothing to know and no one to know it.* At other times the clouds of delusion and the pressing mind states were too much to deal with and I would just lie there motionless, in misery.

Unable to turn over and having nothing to look at but that large, white clock, I was mesmerized by the sound and movement of the second hand. I was desperate to be released to my room on the seventh floor, my room with a window and a view of the outside world. I longed to watch the clouds and see the sky. I wondered whether I would ever see the sky again.

I made an attempt to convince the doctors on their next visit that I was strong enough to be released to my former room. When the ICU doctor and his young assistant came in that day, they asked me how I was doing. I pulled myself up onto my elbows, supporting my head and upper back for the first time in more than a week, and said, "I'm really surprised how strong I feel today, Doc." It took all the strength I had to stay propped up for a few seconds until they left the room.

As he opened the door to leave, I heard the doctor say to his assistant, "He does look strong today, doesn't he?" It wasn't until I noticed his raised eyebrows and slight smile that I realized he was kidding. I fell onto my back feeling discouraged. I wanted, needed, to believe it could be so. Then I looked at myself—tubes coming into me from all over the place, blood pressure and blood oxygen level machines hooked up, oxygen mask with horns attached—struggling to prop up my head. It was not going to be easy to convince these people that I could hold my own if given the chance.

I earnestly wanted that chance. I chanted, several times a day with my hands pressed palm-to-palm. Then I exercised. Lifting my arms and legs ten times each and doing reps several times per hour was my attempt to increase my strength so as to find a way out of this hellish realm. It was the first time since I had been admitted that I felt there was something I could do to help myself, and this gave me a sense of satisfaction. I exercised for a few minutes whenever I had the stamina. It may be the toughest workout I'll ever do, I thought, but I am going to have to find a way out of here. Raise the leg ten times, the other leg, raise the left arm. . . . If I give up now it may be the respirator again, and who knows if I'll ever get off it the next time.

To my horror the exertion caused me to spit up volumes of blood. I buzzed the nurse and informed her. She was not alarmed and told me that my lungs had been bleeding for some time and that coughing up blood was a good sign. With my platelets so low, it was unavoidable that I would have bleeding of the lungs from pneumonia and having spent all that time on the respirator.

"It's okay to keep exercising," she said. "The quicker you clear your lungs, the sooner you'll be able to go back to your room."

Music to my ears. It was probably a good thing that I had very little energy, because I have been known to overdo things at times. I was becoming acquainted with this new body and was grateful just to be able to move again. I wanted to proceed carefully. It was going to be slow, attentive progress for now.

The next day the doctors told me that there were no signs of the blast cells that indicate leukemia. They would wait a few more days for the conclusive test. If my blood counts continued to improve, and if I could hold my own on oxygen without the respirator, I could return to my room upstairs.

My hopes soared and I began looking forward to escaping ICU soon. Then Margaret came in with upsetting news. I had developed another infection and the move to the seventh floor was going to be delayed. For the first time in days I became aware of the immense weight of my body. I seemed to weigh a ton and was sinking fast. I knew I was facing serious discouragement and depression. Many times in retreats I had faced that downward spiral and I knew the dangers of giving in to dark mind states. I needed to act quickly because I had so little energy left and it would take every bit of it to stay positive.

"Please tell the doctor I want to see him," I said to Margaret.

The doctor was young and handsome, well dressed and sporting a colorful silk tie. After he introduced himself, I asked, "Are you married yet, Doc?"

"No, not yet. Why do you ask?"

"I just wanted to warn you: you soon will be."

He laughed and asked why I thought so.

"You're a doctor, young, good looking, and you have great

taste in ties," I replied. "You haven't got a chance." We all had a chuckle. Then I became serious.

"Doc, I can't take this room anymore. I need something to eat, and for goodness' sake, why won't they give me a drink? I'm going nuts. I don't think I can take it anymore."

His first suggestion was Prozac to help me deal with my depression. I told him that I was normally a very positive individual and that I was not feeling depressed. It was just that I needed a break from that room, a small drink, and something light to eat.

"Then," I said, "I can get on with the fight—morale is getting awfully low in here and I have nothing left to offer."

He left the room and consulted Margaret. To my surprise they returned with a cup of tea, a bowl of ice cream, and a bowl of chocolate pudding.

"We're going to send you up to the seventh floor tonight, Mr. Bedard," he said.

Tears of joy ran down my face. It was a celebration of life. The doctor, a few nurses from the ward, Margaret, and my mother all stood about the room staring at me, sharing in my joy. I looked to the nurse and said, "Did you notice? I've been complaining, begging, and pleading for a drink for days with no results, but I give this guy one compliment on his great-looking tie and look . . . ice cream, pudding, and ahhh . . . a cup of tea. Man, have I been talking to the wrong people!" Facing many teary-eyed, smiling faces, I indulged.

Although I had never tasted ice cream in tea before, I put all the vanilla ice cream in my tea and feasted on the best treat I have ever had. I don't think I can remember having a finer meal in my entire life.

The doctor had told Margaret that he thought I should remain in ICU for a few more days but that if I gave up the fight at this point it could be very serious. They agreed that a move back to my room would provide a morale boost and hoped that I would not have to return to ICU. If I did, it would be after a psychological break and some emotional rest.

Back in my old room again, the tube through my nose into my stomach and a couple of the intravenous lines were removed. I hadn't realized how much these tubes hurt and how uncomfortable they were until they were being taken out.

The curtain was open and I took in the sky in all its glory. There was a great sense of satisfaction and a feeling of having come home. I looked at my mother and said, "I can die now, Mom."

"Please don't talk like that, honey!" she responded. "You're going to get through this, and in a year's time we will all get together and have a party to celebrate." I wished I could believe her, but I really didn't know if I'd be alive to see the next day.

The rest of that evening was spent calling my children, my father, my brothers and sisters, and my Zen teacher to let them know I was out of ICU. Inevitably, after their surprise at hearing my voice there were tears of joy and then admonitions for me to rest because I sounded so weak. In the months that followed I developed a great respect for the sound of the human voice. I began to listen more carefully to others'. Although my voice did not seem to fluctuate much to me, my friends and loved ones could almost always tell how I was doing by the sound of my voice.

I slept very little again that night. Inability to sleep was a problem that persisted throughout my illness.

One of the greatest things about being out of ICU was that now my friends could visit me again. A day seldom went by without Ian, Ross, or Randy coming in with coffee, smiles and hugs, pictures of our cabin, and news of the Zen Centre. Sometimes they just sat quietly with me while I rested.

My second day back in my room turned out to be an emotional roller coaster for my mom and me. Margaret had returned home to check on the children and run some errands. In the morning a resident doctor entered my room and told me that he was going to do a bone marrow aspiration to test for leukemia cells. Of all the aspirations I have had, this one proved to be the worst. First the doctor had trouble giving the local anesthetic. Then he had such a difficult time inserting the needle into the pelvis that I cried out in pain. He apologized and continued digging into the pelvis, trying to find the soft, spongy marrow. Finally he managed to draw the necessary amount of marrow and took it to the lab. He left me sweating and defeated in an empty room.

My family was waiting to see me. I needed and longed for their support, yet no one came in. They had been told by the nurses that I needed to rest after such a difficult test. Eventually I settled down and began to relax. Within minutes the door opened and the infectious-disease specialist came in to discuss my internal bleeding. From my neck down to the breast I was black and blue, as was one shoulder. He was there with his assistant to take more blood samples. Now I was really scared.

About an hour after they left, the specialist's young assistant came to tell me that they had targeted the infection and that they had an antibiotic to help control this specific bacteria. My mom and I shared a joyous hug when we heard the good news. My mom reassured me that she knew all along that her prayers were going to be answered and that I was going to get well. I was not so easily convinced. Yet a glimmer of hope began to emerge in my heart. I did not want the good news to take me to lofty heights, as I knew how hard the fall could be. Nonetheless, I was raised.

Within an hour the assistant was again standing at the foot of my bed, this time with a long face. He simply said, "Mr. Bedard, I'm sorry. The infection we identified was for the fellow across the hall, not you. I'm sorry I was mistaken."

Then he was gone again. I sunk deep into my sheets trying to disappear. Not wanting my mother to see my disappointment or the tears in my eyes, I turned my face away from her. When I did look back to reassure her that I was okay, she too was looking away, teary eyed. I have heard people speak of how alone they feel when suffering, and I have experienced this myself. It is the terrible lonely truth at times. This was not one of those times. This illness was as much my mother's that day as it was mine, much as on those nights when I was bathed in cold cloths by my brothers and sisters, or on the "socks on, socks off" nights with Margaret. My wife, my family, my Zen teacher, my friends, my sangha, and my relatives were all suffering from leukemia.

The infectious-disease specialist came in to encourage me. He said that it was not uncommon for infections to remain unidentified and that it was more the norm. He said they would continue to use the shotgun effect and just keep hitting me with random antibiotics until something worked. My mom and I felt a little better knowing that I might not have to return to ICU.

After having been so encouraged—"We have targeted the infection"—then so crestfallen—"Sorry, I was mistaken"—I was feeling a need to coast emotionally. Just holding on was all I could handle at the moment, but the roller-coaster ride was not yet over. The next time the nurse came into my room to check my blood pressure and my blood oxygen level she rushed out and returned with the doctor.

"Jim," the doctor said, "your blood oxygen level is dropping too quickly. We're going to have to send you back to ICU. It's really what's best."

I was too weak to sound convincing, but I replied, "Doc, I'm not going back down there. I'm gonna make it or break it in this bed. Is that clear? I'm not ready to go back down there, not yet."

They increased my oxygen intake and left me to think about my decision. The doctor on call left the room not knowing what to do with me and went to phone my hematologist. I sat up in bed for the first time since being sedated in ICU and said, "Mom, please help me get these covers off."

"Oh my goodness, honey, what are you doing? Please, let's just go back downstairs. It may only be for a day or two. You've come so far." All the while she was helping me remove the covers. "What on earth are you doing?" she asked.

I was lying on my back kicking my feet in a bicycle peddling motion. My arms were extended from my sides, and I was bringing them up and down from the sides of my bed to above my chest, then down again, keeping my feet peddling all the while.

"I'm fighting, Mom," I cried, with tears running down my face. "I'm fighting the only way I know how. I'll beat this thing—I'll increase the oxygen level. You can be sure I'll spend tonight in this bed one way or another."

I heard a slight whisper, "Oh my poor boy! God help him."

The exercise was causing me to cough a lot and I hoped that was good, as lots of blood was being ejected from my lungs. Neither of us really knew if what I was doing was helping or not, but we both sensed that my spirits had changed.

Within the next hour the nurse said that my lungs were clearing enough and that they would delay the trip to the ICU ward and just keep me on a higher level of oxygen. She made me promise not to keep anything from her, but from fear of being sent back to ICU, I had not told anyone of the chills and fever I had developed. I was so determined not to return to that ward. The nurse won my trust when she convinced me that she was the very one who could keep me on the seventh floor. From then on, I felt that she was working with me. She became my coach on how to proceed and I confided in her.

A few hours passed and the resident, the same doctor who had had such a hard time with the bone marrow aspiration that morning, visited my room.

"Jim, I have good news for you," he said. "The results of your bone marrow aspiration from this morning are good." He placed his hand on mine and said, "You, my friend, are in remission. Congratulations, you are a very lucky man!" We then shook hands and I burst into tears.

When I was first diagnosed, we were told that my odds of my

surviving were approximately 15 percent, and I knew that about 40 percent of all those diagnosed with AML leukemia never make it to their first remission. It was the first time since I had been admitted to the hospital that I actually thought it might be possible for me to survive the disease.

"Mom, did you hear that?" I said. "Maybe I'll be home for Thanksgiving after all."

"Yes, isn't that wonderful! Don't worry, honey, you'll be home for Thanksgiving."

I spent the rest of the night on the phone calling Margaret, my family, Sensei, and my dear friends, sharing the good news. It had been quite a day.

"Mom," I said, "remember that verse I recited for you before I went into ICU: 'If your mind is not clouded with unnecessary things,/No season is too much for you.' Well, another Zen master put it this way, 'Every day is a good day.' He was trying to help us understand that if we enter into every aspect of our life fully, then we won't cling to ideas of good and bad, high and low. When we live like that, we see that in every situation things are just as they are. We've certainly had our share of highs and lows today, haven't we, Mom? Wasn't today a good day?"

With tear-stained cheeks and a soft smile she replied, "Yes, indeed, honey, today was a good day."

4

KARMA

Chance is a word void of sense;
Nothing can exist without a cause.

—VOLTAIRE

THE NEXT MORNING, Wednesday, September 13, Margaret and
my mother arrived smiling and refreshed. I too had slept relatively
well for the first time since leaving the ICU. I felt stronger and
knew that the fever was gone. My mom and Margaret told me that
my father would be returning soon. He hadn't seen me in more
than a week.

"Dad's coming? How bad do I look?" I asked. "Please tell me
the truth." My mom said I looked great, but Margaret said that I
needed a little work. They sponge-bathed me and helped me into
clean pajamas and a robe.

My father was having a very hard time seeing his son so helpless.
I'm sure it was no worse for him than for the rest of my family
and friends, but his frustration was different. Over the years we
had come to rely on him as Mr. Fix It. It didn't matter whether it
was fixing a broken doll or installing new sinks and shelves, he
was the one who could solve the problem. My sister had found
him crying outside my room when I was in ICU saying, "I should

be able to fix this, you know—damn it, that's what I do. I fix things."

My mom and Margaret left to buy me an electric razor and a comb. The nurses would not allow me to use a blade to shave, concerned that I might nick myself. With my platelets so low, bleeding was a serious danger. To my surprise, when I tried to comb my hair, large clumps fell out onto the bed and my robe. Although I had been warned well in advance, I had forgotten about that part. It was not traumatic for me though. In Buddhism, ordained people shave their heads as a symbol of renouncing their attachments to the world. While I had never been bald before, I felt that to some degree or another I, too, had renounced everything.

With serious illness one is quickly stripped naked for all to see. The different masks we hide behind dissolve. All I identified with as my self was breaking up and dispersing. I was experiencing the truth of the Buddha's teachings of impermanence firsthand. I had been robbed of my cherished health in a matter of a couple short weeks. My good reputation at the company I worked for meant nothing now. Decades of eating well, exercising, doing yoga, conscientious work habits, daily meditation, all were gone. Here I lay, very thin, applying for a disability pension, and unable even to sit up in bed. I had no guarantee of a future, my past identity had been eradicated, and the present was demanding one hundred percent of my attention.

However grim that sounds, I was now free. Free from myself. Free from that drive for perfection. Free from attachments to ideas of who and what I was or should be. The slate had been wiped clean. The leukemia had forced me to live in the present, here and now. This is the way of Zen: the ever changing entity called "myself" responding fully to conditions of the moment, flowing from one thing to the next.

Illness released me from idealizing my health, status, body, and states of mind. The leukemia was there, I felt, to heal another, much deeper sickness that I would never have recognized without its help: the sickness of pain-producing behavior and habit patterns stemming from seeds that were planted lifetimes ago. The reason for this illness was not a mystery to me. Like all Buddhists, I clearly understood the answer to the question, What did I do to deserve this? It was obvious: my own karma brought me to this point.

It is hard to describe how liberating this understanding was. At the same time, it made me feel vulnerable. My thoughts, speech, and action, everything, had an effect. Unfortunately, my habit energies continued to exert a strong influence on my life, making it difficult for me to live as I would like. Invariably, behaviors that lead to pain and suffering for others lead to pain and suffering for oneself. "Pain follows pain as surely as the wheel follows the footsteps of the ox," the Buddha said.

Before long I would become aware of the deeper karma underlying my illness. One may think that it requires great psychic powers to see into past karma, but when the Buddha was asked about seeing into one's past, he simply told his disciples, "Look at yourself now." Our past is reflected as clearly as though in a mirror, manifesting itself in the present. This moment is as it is because of past causes, and in turn, is the cause of future effects. "If you want to see your future," the Buddha also said, "look at yourself now." Our body and circumstances are the memory of our past actions stemming from body, speech, and mind.

No guilt or anger accompanied the awareness of how I came to be so ill. Instead there was a clear sense of responsibility and a real sense of urgency. I knew I needed to proceed very carefully, since I was the architect of my own life and future lives. There was no one else to blame, no one else to hold responsible. Looking back I saw a path that led to the present, a path that I had freely chosen to walk. An ancient Chinese saying came to mind: "If you are not careful, you just might end up in the direction you are headed."

My outlook stood in sharp contrast to the way of looking at suffering that I saw in some brochures containing spiritual advice for cancer patients. One writer said that questioning the why of our suffering leads to anger and despair, and eventually this anger spills over into our relationships with our loved ones and into our relationship with God. I strongly disagree. I have learned that the practice of introspection while ill combined with a belief in karma can lead to insight, acceptance, and peace, even in the most difficult of times.

Having spent years reflecting on the law of causation, I found it jarring to hear hospital clergy begin their visits by saying, "Jim, we don't have answers to the questions of why God chooses some to suffer and not others, but—" I would stop them immediately. "I feel differently about that. In Buddhism all things have their cause. Our body is a memory of our past deeds. Karma . . ."

Just as one can tell from the leaves of a tree the type of seed that was planted years earlier, an open and honest look into our present circumstances can lead to insight into their causes. We create our own suffering, and the teachings we need most lie within that suffering. There can be no lasting peace until we have dealt with all past karma, "good" or "bad." We are the inheritors of our past actions, and this life presents us with a wonderful opportunity to meet their effects with a bow of acceptance. Leukemia has left me a gift for which I am immensely grateful: the resolve to examine my own thoughts, words, and deeds carefully and to try to live each day in harmony with all sentient beings.

When my dad arrived, he broke into tears. Even though he had been warned, it was a shock for him to see me so thin, pale, and bald. I hadn't seen myself in a mirror since being admitted to ICU and wasn't aware of how much my body had deteriorated. My dad came over to my bed and hugged and kissed me. This was unusual for him. He grew up during a time when it was more appropriate for men to shake hands than to hug or kiss each other.

I smiled and said, "Gee, Dad, have you ever kissed a bald-headed man before?"

"No, son, but I will, I will," he said while sobbing. We again hugged, and had a great visit.

My dad's awareness of his own health and the health of his children took on a whole new meaning. All of us developed a new appreciation for life, realizing it to be so precious and so frail, entering into each moment with newfound wonder. Sometimes late at night one of my brothers or sisters could be heard apologizing to another for some transgression that had taken place years before, or someone else would tell a sibling or a parent that he really didn't say "I love you" enough. We were all thrust into the truth of life's impermanence and did not want to miss one precious moment.

That day the sores in my throat made it too painful even to speak. Eating and drinking were out of the question, although I was now allowed to do both. The first meal I ordered was spinach lasagna, salad, and a vanilla milkshake. It looked so good, but all I could do was enjoy the aroma. There I sat skinny, hungry, thirsty, and unable to indulge. A hungry ghost for sure.

When the doctors came they were concerned that I was fading away so quickly. They told me I should start eating. I explained that I couldn't and they decided to put me on morphine to ease the pain so that I could eat. The morphine only caused me to vomit relentlessly. As there had been little in my stomach for many days, a bright green film of bile spattered over my bed, pajamas, and robe.

Margaret spent the next few days and nights at my bedside, sleeping in a chair and getting me Popsicles whenever I felt I could get one past my throat. We canceled all visitors, and I just vegetated. Salt water or baking soda rinses would have prevented the sores from spreading, but I had been unconscious when they were forming. Now I had to sit with the pain. There were gashes in the sides and roof of my mouth that I could insert the end of my tongue into—of course, from the inside they felt larger than life. They continued down my throat and covered my tongue and lips.

For the next few days I ate little or nothing and drank only a few drops at a time.

One day Ross was visiting. I said to him, "Look at me, my friend. I'm so skinny and so weak."

Ross asked, "Well, Jim, how does it feel for someone who has always been so strong and fit to be so skinny and weak?"

His question stunned me, although I might have expected it. Ross is a psychologist who counsels cancer patients, and he doesn't shy away from asking tough questions. After the initial surprise, I found his words helpful. It was the first time someone had actually acknowledged to me that I looked like hell. Margaret, my mother, and the rest of my family told me constantly that I looked great. Of course to them, I looked much better than I had when they visited me in ICU.

I thought about his question for a moment, then said, "You know, Ross, I understand that this is my karma. And yet, there is also a part of me, part of everyone, that cannot get sick. It seems to me that deep in our center one can always get in touch with a great tranquillity that is not influenced by the comings and goings of this world. I think most of us have experienced at some time in our lives an inner peace that comes from not identifying too strongly with the passing states of the body-mind."

In contrast to Ross, another person who came to see me said, "Not to worry Jim, life is all an illusion anyway." I did not find this helpful at all. While I was in the hospital, there were many days when this illusory life of mine was filled with pain. When one is suffering, there is suffering. Anyone who really understands that life is an illusion would never say those words to a person who was in pain. True wisdom stems from the realization of the interconnectedness of all things: we no longer see others as outside ourselves. Their pain is our pain; their hunger, our hunger; their thirst, ours as well. While this person might have thought his words reflected great wisdom, without compassion there is no wisdom. Isn't this what Jesus meant when he said, "Love thy neighbor as thyself"?

The healthy can sometimes be unintentionally callous toward the sick. Before I became ill, when I was told that a smoker had developed lung cancer, I would sometimes think, "What a shame, she really shouldn't have smoked so much." If I heard of a friend who had heart problems, I might think, "Well, if only he had taken better care of himself." Even though I would feel deeply for their suffering, my perspective alienated me from them. This illness has helped me see into the cold and insensitive nature of these attitudes. Even if someone has smoked, indulged in alcohol, or been a junk food junkie for years, what do I know of his or her reasons for doing so or of the struggle with addiction, guilt, pain, or frustration? Besides, what has any of this to do with my identifying with the suffering of this person? Since my own illness, when I hear of people ailing, I just want to offer a hug or send as much loving energy as I can in their direction.

It is laudable to avoid things that will adversely affect our health. But take it from one who has been there—eating yogurt, yeast, alfalfa sprouts, whole grains; following a vegetarian diet, and getting plenty of exercise—there is no escaping sickness, old age, and death.

All suffering has a cause, and suffering is a terrible thing. I spoke with Sunyana-sensei one night when my body was racked with pain. There was a deep longing in my heart to live a life that would not cause pain to others. "Those who willingly harm others," I told Sensei, "simply haven't suffered enough in their own lives. I cannot fathom why there is so much suffering going on in the world at the hands of others."

"Yes, Jim. You are exactly right," came her reply. "Those who cause so much suffering in the world have not yet felt enough pain. That's one reason it's so excruciating to see people cause pain to others. It is simply impossible not to feel the deepest sorrow for the suffering they themselves will one day, one lifetime, have to undergo. If only they knew! People cause pain to others and because of this, when the time is right, experience pain themselves. Yet so many of them have no idea why they are suffering. What a tormented wheel this is for those who do not understand the law of causation."

Sometimes when I was alone at night, I spent hours struggling to understand the deeper causes of my illness and the suffering I had caused others. The process of examining and letting go, and my discussions with Sensei about expiating karma, helped me find peace during those long, sleepless nights.

One is very vulnerable when seriously ill, and unfortunately some friends and acquaintances had their own ideas, on a more superficial level, of things I might have done wrong and suggested cures to right these wrongs. At one point I told Margaret that I felt as if I were one of the very few people on this planet who did not know how to cure cancer. People encouraged me to try everything from macrobiotics, seaweed, grapes, and megadoses of vitamins to avoiding toothpaste, white flour, all sugar, and even bottled water. A few naturopathic experts suggested that I begin eating meat immediately. Others suggested that the meat I ate before becoming a vegetarian might have been the cause of the problem.

We received literally dozens of books, letters, and cards suggesting new diets, exercises, and mental therapies. One book I received suggested that cancer was caused by suppressed guilt or anger. To me, this attitude seemed to foster guilt and confusion that was not there to begin with. It was very different from my understanding of the law of causation. Looking at illness from the viewpoint of karma helped me realize that the contributing factors to my sickness extended over countless lifetimes and encompassed innumerable actions of body and speech, as well as states of mind. The doctrine of karma can help those who are suffering understand illness and see it as a period of development. It doesn't help to feel guilty. It is more important to focus on how we choose to work through the karma that is ripening.

Sitting up one night, having barely enough strength to hold a book, let alone to actually read one, I asked Margaret to collect all the information we had received and hide it somewhere. "Margaret," I said, "I really don't know if I'll be alive long enough to read all this stuff."

I realized that these suggestions came from a genuine willingness to help. Yet, I was recovering from a devastating illness and was barely able to sip soup or eat mashed potatoes. All this advice only added to my stress and confusion.

It was very interesting, even a bit comical, when a couple of distant relatives sent their best wishes for my recovery. They had been heavy smokers for more than forty years and were quite obese. It seemed to me they lived on pork sandwiches and Twinkies. Years earlier, I had given them much advice about including more fiber and vegetables in their diets and letting up on cigarettes, but my admonitions fell on deaf ears. Now I was receiving a taste of my own medicine with this mountain of unsolicited advice.

Recently, when Margaret was attending a family reunion, several of our aunts, uncles, and distant relatives—some now in their eighties— approached her with canes in hand and asked about my health. When Margaret returned home to tell me of their inquiries, I was genuinely touched. We were seldom in contact with most of these relatives, and I was, in fact, surprised to hear that some of them were still alive given their health practices for so many decades.

The body is so resilient, I thought. "Margaret," I said, "I don't think we have to worry about the bottled water or the toothpaste." A ton of weight seemed to lift from my shoulders, and my mind became free of the persistent questions regarding what I might have done or might still be doing wrong regarding my health.

Other people had suggested that life had cheated me, but I had no such feelings. The quality of life my discipline and health habits afforded me was far too rich for me to be obsessed about quantity.

Some thought it was "quality"—indulgences—that I had given up for the long-term goal of living to a ripe old age. Nothing could have been further from the truth. I simply tried then, as I do now, to live each day to the fullest. I have no regrets.

By the third week in September, I was strong enough to get out of bed and climb into a wheelchair. My doctor told me that my white blood cells were climbing and that when they reached a certain level I would be able to leave my room. For me this did not mean nearly as much as it did to some patients I met. It was not uncommon to see people standing at their door waiting to get the okay to venture out into the hall. One fellow had us laughing as he danced down the hall hugging the nurses and singing out loud. He was so happy to be out of the confining grip of isolation.

Isolation forces us to be with our self, often under the worst of conditions. For me, isolation did not feel confining now that I had a window in my room and was getting stronger. I could also raise my bed slightly and do some informal zazen. For many years I had sat in meditation facing a wall. It can be said that during meditation, especially during retreats, we sit facing ourselves. One is left to deal with whatever comes up, and there is no turning away or escaping. Of course, at retreats one can visit one's teacher several times a day to ask for guidance.

The practice that seemed to help most when I was nauseated or in pain was the practice of introspection. Looking into "Who and what am I?" at any given moment allowed me to be completely present. Fortunately for me, isolation outside the ICU was not oppressive.

A barber came to shave my head. Losing hair continuously was messy and posed a risk of infection to my Hickman exit site, which was still black from internal bleeding. Soon my platelets and red and white blood cells were climbing steadily, and I was given permission to leave my room. I could now stand on my own well enough to get around a bit. The first time I entered the bathroom,

I was startled to see a pale, skinny old man with sunken eyes looking back from the mirror, bald as a cue ball. No wonder people
are telling me to eat, I thought to myself. I had aged twenty years.

It was clear to me now why several visitors did not recognize
me at first and others were shocked to see me. Even I was startled
by my own reflection. One look encouraged me to do my best to
begin sipping the nutritional shakes I was offered at mealtimes.

The afternoon following my climb into the wheelchair I left my
room for the first time. It was exciting to see the hospital and meet
other patients. As Margaret wheeled me out of my room backward,
I noticed the empty bed where I had spent the last several weeks.
It looked eerie and inviting at the same time. Again the realization
of the impermanence of all things struck me. "Even if I am cured
of leukemia, I will be coming back to this bed," I said to Margaret.
"This bed beckons us all. My trip away from this bed may be long
or short, but someday I will again be returning to this bed."

It was amazing when I looked into the faces of those watching
me. It was, as Sensei had said many times, as if people thought
that only others were going to die, as if I alone were sick and they
were impervious to old age, sickness, and death. A strange feeling
of gratitude for the realization of my own impermanence was with
me that afternoon, and it continues to influence me daily.

Again, Siddhartha's question when he saw the dead person came
to mind, "Are there other instances of this in the world?"

"All who begin life must end it. There is no escaping old age,
sickness, and death," he was told.

Since that day I have often sat with an awareness of death. Sometimes at the beginning of a round of sitting, I imagine the flames
of the crematorium finding their way through the pine box and
consuming my body. I remind myself not to be lax, then I return
again to the question, Who am I at this moment? I resolve not to
become attached to fluctuating emotions and ideas or to this transient body.

Often when weak and confined to bed I would take the Three

Refuges. Taking refuge in Buddha, I placed my hands together at face level as a sign of respect. With palms still together, I lightly touched my lips, taking refuge in dharma, in reverence for the teachings of Buddha. Taking refuge in sangha, I placed my hands over my heart to remind me of all those who suffer and in gratitude for all the help I have received from so many, many people. For me, taking the Three Refuges goes hand in hand with the practice of questioning "Who am I?"

My physiotherapist came to tell me that I would be going down to the gym for therapy that day. I was delighted. We went through the usual ritual of transferring the pumps and intravenous bags from the bed to the wheelchair, and I was off.

What an adventure! Seeing other people crowding the halls, smelling the coffee shops and doughnuts and food from the cafeteria as we passed, and getting a glimpse of the outside world. Even the elevator ride was like that first time as a child when you are so acutely aware of gravity's fluctuating pulls on the body. I was like a kid on his first visit to toyland. Everything shone with clarity and newness.

In the gym I was placed on a large mat and handed some weights. I started with a two-pound weight on each ankle. Kidding with the therapist, I asked her to close the curtains so that no one from my health club could see me if they happened by.

Next came the bench press. As I lay flat on my back I was given a walking cane with a two-pound wrist weight taped to the middle of it and asked to do ten reps. This was certainly a lot less than the 175-pound weights I had lifted not all that long ago. Feeling I could surely handle a little more, we agreed to add another 5 pounds. There I lay struggling with a 7-pound bench press. Instead of being discouraged by my obvious weakness, I found it quite amusing to be struggling with such a light weight. *You've been too strong for too long,* I told myself, remembering I had often taken my good health for granted. *This will help you identify with the less fortunate.*

I looked about at the other patients and realized that none was as frail as I. Men, women, and teenagers were working a leg or an arm, or struggling with light weights. Across the room a thin, elderly woman was peddling a stationary bicycle. *What exuberance!* I thought.

As I lay there in the gym, I remembered the afternoon that Margaret had wheeled me down to the lounge to watch the news on TV. *The media has it all wrong,* I thought. My view of mankind differed considerably from the pictures presented on the news. With all the good around us, it seemed too bad to focus on all the terrible happenings in the world. My family and I were getting help from so many different directions that I could not contain my gratitude. We received visits and cards from old acquaintances, and monetary aid from the Buddhist community, friends, and family. Our children called several times to say that when they returned home from school there were boxes of groceries waiting on our porch without even a note to say who they were from.

I was so humbled. I couldn't keep from thinking, *I am just one of many sick people. How is it that we are receiving so much help?* When I heard about all the chanting services and ceremonies that were being done on my behalf, I could only feel unworthy. In time, though, I became comfortable with these spiritual offerings. I had experienced the power and the clarity of their saving grace and I knew that as all beings are fundamentally connected, all beings in all realms were surely benefiting from these practices. From that point on, I encouraged others to do whatever they could, whenever they could, to help.

There in the hospital gym where I was lifting two-pound leg weights, music was playing in the background. The song "The Road Is Long" came on. I thought of my family, my Zen teacher, and our many friends who had all been so generous and kind. When I heard the words "He ain't heavy, he's my brother," I broke down and cried. Others in the room pretended not to notice, thinking, perhaps, that I was having a rough time. It really didn't matter to me what they thought. I was so full of love and gratitude.

It was truly a moment of grace. There are few times in this life that I have felt so much joy from being so loved.

I enjoyed the immediacy of learning to walk again. What a wonderful experience, the simple joy of just being able to walk upon this earth. Attentive walking embodies the universe.

Margaret and Shirley-Anne bribed me into walking farther each day. If I wanted to ride in the wheelchair, I first had to walk to the chair. Each time they placed the chair farther from my bed, until I was walking out into the hall and eventually down to the lounge. I found the walks wonderful and looked forward to being able to get out of bed several times a day. Soon I longed to venture farther, and we took the elevator down a few floors to wander through the main entrance area. The stroll through the seventh-floor halls did not pass by any outside windows, and I found the change of view on the main floor stimulating.

People look at the sick differently than they do the healthy. I know that now. Normally when I was healthy, I would meet countless smiles and greetings. Now, as I ventured out from my room skinny, weak, and completely bald, without even eyebrows or eyelashes, leaning on my IV pole and longing to interact with others, I was ignored. Even nurses, doctors, and staff often avoided eye contact with me in case their stares should cause me embarrassment. I disappeared into the background, became invisible in the crowded hallways, just one of many patients needing and wanting company. In a bustling building in downtown Toronto, struggling to avoid being knocked over by others, I felt painfully alone.

It was almost the end of September. The sores in my mouth and throat were worse. Swallowing even little sips was unbearable. At the same time my potassium was so low that I had to take supplements in huge "horse pills" that were a struggle to swallow. Like countless other health-conscious patients, I requested bananas, knowing they were high in potassium. My doctors told me that I would have to eat several bushels of bananas to correct the imbalances caused by the drugs I was on. I wrestled with the pills and at times had to request to have them administered intravenously. My throat simply would not allow anything to pass, and when I was able to swallow, I would vomit the bit of fluid that had taken so much effort to get down.

My platelet levels were slow to climb and this concerned us all. The medical team had promised me a week at home before the onset of the next chemo treatment, but they were not about to let me leave until my counts were up. When my hematologist came to see me, I told him that I was concerned about the next bout of chemo.

"Doc," I said, "just before I came in here, I could have run ten miles and canoed all day. I was strong. The last round of chemo almost killed me. What will happen if you hit me again? I'm afraid I don't have the strength for more chemo. A week is not going to be enough time. Please let's negotiate a little more time off before the next treatment."

He replied, "The difficulties you encountered that first time were due to your serious infections and advanced leukemia. For this second treatment, remember that you are in remission. We will again keep you in isolation and do our best to help you avoid infections and pneumonia. I really don't expect it to be as bad this next time around. However, you should know that the next treatment will be stronger and more toxic than the first induction therapy. Any time you undergo chemotherapy there is a chance that it could kill you. Still, this treatment is essential to keep you in remission. If you decide to go ahead with a bone marrow transplant, your odds will be much better if you are still in your first remission. I don't want to take a chance of a relapse. AML moves too fast."

I posted a graph on the wall showing my platelet, hemoglobin, and white blood cell counts, as well as my temperature and medications for each day. My visitors would carefully examine the day's climb or fall as they entered the room. Hospital staff, nurses, and doctors all glanced at my counts before asking me how I was doing. Slowly but surely the red and white cells and platelets all climbed to levels that were considered safe, and I was given the okay to go home for a week. I felt insecure and vulnerable. The outside world seemed too big and too busy, and I didn't know where I would fit in or who I had become.

When I was packing to leave, I was surprised to find that all I had to wear were shorts and a T-shirt. When I had rushed into St. Mike's that warm August afternoon, I had not planned to stay for more than a couple of weeks, and I was leaving on a cold, windy day in October.

The elevator ride down to the first floor was about all I could handle. Feeling very nauseated and almost vomiting, I stumbled out the front door wondering what the heck I was doing leaving the secure surroundings of the hospital. With my parents on either side and Margaret behind me, I stood looking at the traffic and busy sidewalks, feeling the way I imagine the elderly often feel.

"Dad," I said, "please make sure no one bumps into me. I don't know if I can get up if I fall."

"Don't worry, son," came the reply. "No one's going to run into you."

A reversal in roles. My parents, in their mid-sixties, were getting used to feeling more secure when their children were with them. This was a déjà vu of earlier times when they held my hands and were delighted to see me taking those first few steps.

It was wonderful to be in a car again riding through the countryside. The fall colors were just beginning to light up the hills, and the flowing yellow grasses and fields of wildflowers seemed to roll on endlessly. Stacks of hay reminded me of the cold, brutal months ahead. *How will I ever get ready?* I thought.

When we arrived home, banners of WELCOME HOME DAD and WE LOVE YOU DAD greeted me. Tears ran down my face and I knew why The Wizard of Oz had always been one of my favorite movies. It was so good to be home again!

After I was greeted by my children, everyone entered the kitchen from our back porch. Everyone except me, that is. There was a step up into the kitchen and it was unmanageable for the weak, sunken-eyed man who had returned from the hospital. It was clear to us all that the person standing at the entrance to our kitchen was very different from the one who had passed through this doorway just over five weeks before.

"How will I ever get up the steps to go to the bathroom?" I asked.

No sooner had the words left my lips than I noticed my father measuring the stairs and making plans for the railings he would install the next morning. My Mr. Fix-It dad finally had something to fix. He was in his element and spent the day repairing the many things, large and small, that needed it around the house.

Nights at home were no more restful than those in the hospital. The drugs I was on still interfered with my sleep. There were so many different types and doses and times that I had to make a list for each hour of the day. I thought about the numerous possible side effects—swelling, headaches, hair growth in unusual places, bone damage, liver damage, and kidney damage. If I experience even a small percentage of these side effects, what will I be like then? I wondered.

Pain in my stomach and throat continued to be a problem. I survived on mashed potatoes and creamed corn, which I couldn't taste. The chemo had temporarily destroyed all but my bitter taste buds. When I grew tired of bland foods, I feasted on a half jar of olives. I don't know how nutritious my diet was, those few weeks, but it didn't seem to matter anymore.

With not much to do all day, mealtime became an important event—a meaningful, sometimes exciting change in my oversimplified life. I developed a new appreciation for the simple pleasure of eating.

Within a few days of being home, I craved beets big-time. Margaret managed to find a neighbor who had some homegrown and we made beet-top tea. As I sat looking out our kitchen window at the farmer's field next door, I was surprised to find my heart so at peace and contented. Sitting there wondering why I was not depressed, I sipped my beet-top tea and then asked for assistance to make it down the few stairs to my zendo. Once inside, I offered incense and made a standing bow of gratitude facing the figures I had sat with that first night after returning from the emergency room in Peterborough.

It seemed as if that ceremony had taken place lifetimes ago. My heart was full of gratitude for all the help I had received over the past month. As I stood there on weakened legs with hands pressed palm-to-palm, I felt whole. Although skinny, pale, weak, and in pain, I felt complete. There was nothing lacking. A clarity and tranquillity had entered me that evening that was to become my refuge in the trying times ahead. A tear rolled down my cheek and I whispered, "How could I possibly have done this, be doing this, without your help." My Zen teacher, the sangha, my family and friends, the buddhas and bodhisattvas, I hoped, would feel my words. My gratitude seemed to merge with all the help I was receiving.

A nurse came every day. At first I was quite nervous with these new nurses. Their protocol was different from what I was accustomed to, and it was obvious they did not have experience with procedures such as flushing a central venous catheter (the Hickman line) or cleaning its exit site. On my second or third day at home a nurse drew two syringes of air from my line. We both became very concerned, almost to the point of panic. If air got into the line and into my heart, it could very well be fatal. A phone call to St. Michael's didn't solve the problem, and Margaret rushed me to the hospital. After that episode I became very involved in the care of my lines and exit site. Within days it was I who walked the home care nurses through the procedures. I was soon tending to the exit site and flushing the lines myself.

One afternoon Amanda and Ray talked me into walking around the neighborhood. It was a beautiful fall day, and I was glad to accommodate them and at least make an attempt. The air was wonderful, the sky magnificent, and the walk slow. I tried not to take notice of the faces peeking from behind the curtains of the houses we passed. It was all I could do to walk supported by Ray and Amanda. Once home, I rested, then called my parents, who had left Bethany the day before, to tell them that I felt strong enough to make the trip to North Bay for Thanksgiving dinner.[1]

Margaret, our children, and I ventured to my parents' home through winding hills blazing with the multitudinous colors of fall in northern Ontario. Although I found the ride enjoyable, I was exhausted, too weak after all to be traveling such a long distance. I went because I really didn't know whether I'd ever again have the chance to sit with my family for a Thanksgiving meal.

During dinner I listened carefully to my family's side of the story of my days in ICU. We had time to share our feelings and support each other. It was moving for me to hear that when I was "out of it" the whole family was dealing with their grief and was suffering a great deal. They described the many tubes and machines I was hooked up to and told me of the liver failure, spleen failure, kidney failure, and so on. Michael jokingly tried to convince me that even my "splucker" organ had failed. I'd been hearing his tall tales far too long to bite at that one.

I couldn't thank them enough for being there for me and for their love and support. It was truly a thanks-giving meal.

"But," I warned everyone, "we are still at the starting gates, and the most difficult phases of this journey lie ahead."

They reassured me that they had the stamina to see me through the next several months or however long it would take. Even though I was beginning to feel more positive about the months that lay ahead, part of me worried that there was no way I could possibly survive another round of chemotherapy.

"Mom," I said, "remember that night of feet bicycling and arm waving? You know, I was only kidding when I said I'd be home for Thanksgiving. I really didn't think I'd make it this far."

"I know, honey," she replied, "I knew you weren't serious and were just trying to comfort your worried mother. But what you didn't know was that I *was* serious! I never doubted for a moment that you'd be home for Thanksgiving."

My Thanksgiving meal consisted of mashed potatoes well moistened with creamed corn and a few olives for dessert. What a fine meal it was!

5

IMPERMANENCE

I know this is the
Final road each of us must
Go along; but I didn't expect
Yesterday was that day for him,
Today for her.

—JAPANESE WAKA POEM

MICHAEL AND MARGARET accompanied me to be readmitted
to St. Michael's Hospital for my second round of chemotherapy.
The wait was long and tiring and I was feeling apprehensive. I was
stepping into the ring like a prizefighter who knows he is not
properly prepared for the bout. I was already defeated.

My doctor had tried to convince me that this next time around
wouldn't be anything like the first, but my body was telling me
otherwise. I found his encouraging words hard to believe. It was
my first day back and already I was exhausted. Once in my room,
I was hooked up to the IV pump. Because it would take a week for
chemotherapy to affect my blood counts, I would not have to be
in isolation until then. The nurse came in to take blood and to let
us know that the chemotherapy would begin the next morning. I
wasn't ready.

As there was no medication scheduled that first evening, I was given permission to be unhooked from the pumps and go out for dinner with Margaret and Mike. Although my sense of taste had not yet returned, the abscesses in my mouth were better and I enjoyed our meal out. Eating in a restaurant with Margaret and my brother was such a normal activity that I felt less afraid.

The next morning my doctor asked about my blood tests and those of my siblings. "Which blood tests?" I asked.

"The ones for blood compatibility to see if you have a bone marrow match in your family. They were supposed to have been completed before you were readmitted."

Through a serendipitous oversight we had not been contacted, and the blood tests were not done. It was good news to me that the chemo would have to wait a few days until after we were all tested. It was important to get good samples of my blood before I was assaulted by the chemotherapy. This was the break I was looking for.

I am fortunate to have five siblings with the same parents, as the odds of finding a match in the public pool are anywhere from one in a thousand to one in five hundred thousand, depending on various factors. The chance of finding a match among full siblings is one in four. Nevertheless, there were no guarantees. Some patients who had only one sister or brother had found a match, and others with much larger families had not.

We called my siblings and they all made plans to come to Toronto for testing within the next few days. I requested a meeting with my hematologist.

"Doc," I said, "I'm going to be in this room for the next five weeks or so. How about disconnecting me from this pump until all the tests are over and treatments begin. That way I can leave the hospital to go out for walks and dinner during the next few days."

He agreed as long as I promised to get plenty of rest and stayed at the hospital overnight. I needed to be available first thing in the mornings for the daily blood test and blood pressure, blood oxygen levels, and temperature readings. I also needed to have my lungs x-rayed and have another bone marrow aspiration.

For the next few days Margaret, Michael, and I were like tourists. In the afternoons and evenings I was free to go out and see the town. My sense of taste was returning, and, oh, how I remember that first meal I actually tasted—angel hair spaghetti covered with a spicy tomato and veggie sauce topped with mounds of Parmesan cheese. I felt ten thousand miles away from the hospital, finally getting the rest and break I needed.

Late the next afternoon the rest of my siblings showed up. Their tests were scheduled for the following morning at a lab where the blood could be tested immediately. Margaret had returned home for a few days to be with the children. She tried to do this each time she knew I had lots of visitors.

Mike and I didn't tell my brothers and sisters about the delay in my chemo treatment. As my strength was improving daily, and they had not seen me for several days, we planned to set them up. I dressed and got ready for dinner and lay under my bedcovers waiting for them to arrive. My doctor had given me permission to leave again that night, but he warned me that it was to be the last time for a while. My blood tests had been completed and chemotherapy was to begin the next morning.

When my siblings arrived, they found me as expected, lying in bed, looking frail. Even though I did feel weak, I was stronger than I let on. They suspected that the chemo was already making me nauseated. As soon as everyone was settled in the room, I threw off the covers, sat up, and said, "Guess what? We're all going out to dinner together!"

The room erupted with cries of joy, laughter, and disbelief.

We visited a restaurant my family had frequented while I was in ICU. Once we were inside and seated, a lull seemed to come over everyone. Then I noticed tears welling up in Eric's eyes. He said, "Remember? Remember what I said about coming here?"

He received a few smiles and questioning looks. Then he turned to face us all and said, "Remember when we were all here the Saturday we were told that Jim wasn't going to make it? I urged us not to give up hope and said that the next time we came here he'd be with us. Well, here we all are, and here he is."

At this we all became teary-eyed. We were so pleased to have this time together. My brothers and sisters were delighted to see me out of bed and acting somewhat normal. Sick as I was, just being out with them in a familiar setting had a precious feeling of ordinariness to it.

"I hope we find a match tomorrow," I said. "The doctors say there is a one-in-four chance that siblings will match, so between the five of you, we should be okay."

"Don't worry," Cindy-Lee said, "one of us is bound to match up. It will probably be me, and if it is, you're very lucky, because I definitely have the best marrow."

"I hope it is you, Cindy. You live well, and after all, you're the youngest. I'm sure I'd feel fifteen years younger with your marrow," I told her.

"Well, if you wake up the morning after the transplant and start chanting, "I take refuge in Bud . . . Hail Mary full of grace," then you'll know for sure I was the donor."

We all broke up with laughter. I said, "Right. And if I wake up holding a deck of cards and doing one-hand shuffles, I'll know Eric was my donor." (Eric is a professional magician and is almost never without a deck of cards in one hand and some coins in the other.)

We joked about the many transformations that were possible depending on who my donor turned out to be. Each of my siblings insisted it would be best for me to have his or her bone marrow. I said, "One thing for sure, though, my IQ will certainly drop twenty or thirty points regardless of whose marrow I receive." My two sisters quickly reassured their brothers that any male receiving a woman's marrow was bound to improve considerably.

We had fun making light of the situation, but beneath it we

could feel the tension. We knew that if no match was found among my siblings the next day, my chances were slim that we would find one in the public pool.

When we had finished eating, I said, "Thank you all so much for coming. Having you here with me tonight has really made a big difference. These past few days have given me the time I needed to prepare myself. We can go back now. I feel ready."

Walking taller than I had since before the whole ordeal began, I made my way back to the hospital, arm in arm with my family. With my spirits more positive and my body stronger, I felt ready to face the challenge.

That night I set up an altar in my room and stood before it with hands in gassho. *I feel so whole, so complete. Why is it, I was wondering, that I am so filled with gratitude? I really don't understand it. Never before in my life have I felt such equanimity.* I was truly at peace with the world. Standing there having just come out of six weeks of the most difficult time of my life and facing another several months of treatment, I was content. A couple of lines from a verse that I had written a few months earlier to Sensei came to mind:

> The past no longer haunting,
> The future no longer obstructing.

There was no past, no future, no life, no death, no one separate from this ever-changing One Mind. I was lifted above the restricting confines of my body-mind. My past efforts in zazen and the contributions of others who were chanting and practicing with me in mind were carrying me through these difficult times.

With tears welling up, I made a standing bow and climbed into bed. Once settled, I sat up, placed my hands palm-to-palm, took the Three Refuges in Buddha, Dharma, and Sangha, and did some informal meditation.

I was still inching my way across a tightrope, not knowing how long I was going to live—days, weeks, months. A fall could come at any moment and death was waiting below to claim the broken body. How most people deal with this type of stress I don't know. For me each time fear would raise its head, I would face it straight on and ask myself again and again, *Who is aware of this fear? Who am I really?* It was this constant looking into Mind that was my saving grace. The penetrating and liberating practice of introspection allowed me refuge from the maelstrom around me.

That evening and so many times since, there was no death before me, no one to die. No birth, no beginning, no end to this Mind. The whole universe was encompassed in that one standing bow, in the sitting done in an inclined bed. I vowed, whether I lived or died, never to forget the wonderful lessons that I was learning through my tribulations. I had paid too dearly for this new-found insight.

Many patients seemed to crumple under the strain. They were often ill-tempered to their visitors and the hospital staff. Their hostility helped remind me to do my utmost never to give in to negative feelings and the anger that can accompany them. Several times when the short-staffed nurses were pressed for time they would visit me at the end of a shift and apologize for not having paid attention to me that day. One nurse told me that a woman down the hall and I were referred to by the nurses as their "good patients," the ones who never complained. She felt it was unfair and unfortunate for us that others received more attention because of their bitterness, misery, and self-assertive manner. I reassured her that those who were demoralized by fear, anger, and other emotions were more in need of their care and support than I was. My heart went out to these patients. Serious illness can be enough to handle without having antagonistic feelings as well. Many patients did not have the faith or spiritual practice to sustain them on this tortuous path.

Even with deep faith, it was not easy dealing with serious illness when I was constantly surrounded by death. A few rooms down from me a fellow died, and his wife and family could be heard crying in the halls. He was my age. Often when it got too noisy the nurses would come by and close the doors to our rooms. They knew how a death on the floor would affect the morale of the other patients. But the emotion could still be felt and the muffled cries would find their way into our rooms anyway. I would often get up and open my door. I did not want to forget. Then I would go to my altar or sit in my bed facing the altar and, with the person who had just passed on in mind, chant the Prajña Paramita.

> . . . No withering, no death, no end of them.
> Nor is there pain or cause of pain . . .
> So know that the bodhisattva,
> holding to nothing whatever
> but dwelling in prajña wisdom,
> is free of delusive hindrance,
> rid of the fear bred by it,
> and reaches clearest nirvana.

The next morning my siblings left early to visit the lab for the blood compatibility test. I was hooked up to the pump and started on chemotherapy. The pumps were a real nuisance, not only because I would now have a "dancing partner" for the next several weeks, but because of their constant humming, clicking, and buzzing.

Over the next few days, perhaps because I was more aware this second time around and not yet in isolation, I met several patients just before they died. Margaret came to the hospital so much that she developed relationships with families of the other patients. Often one of them would join her for coffee or lunch in the cafeteria. She, too, was experiencing death all around her. A few days after my readmittance, the woman in one of the rooms beside me died, and wailing could again be heard in the halls. She was from a large family, and many visitors had come from overseas. Within an hour of her family's arrival, she had wakened, smiled to them all, and was gone.

Margaret was in the hall the next morning talking to a young woman who had the same type of leukemia that I had. She was younger than I, and Margaret was befriending her eleven-year-old son.

"We have a boy your age," she said, "but he's not yet as tall as you are."

Margaret asked the woman how she liked her coffee and headed down to the coffee shop to get some and to get me a sesame-seed bagel smothered with cream cheese and a large deli pickle. Margaret and my family kept pushing these treats on me. They knew I was fond of them and that I needed to put on extra weight. We also knew that I would soon be going without food for weeks.

When Margaret returned with the coffee and bagel, she was greeted by a nurse and a distraught little boy standing alone in the hall. His mother had died.

Margaret entered my room in disbelief. We both wanted to help the child, but one of the nurses and the hospital chaplain were there with him until his father and grandparents could arrive. A nurse came in and began to hook up my first bag of chemotherapy for that day. An eerie feeling came over me, knowing as I did that it was often this "cure" that was killing some of my fellow patients. There was no forgetting that we weren't out of the woods yet and that my chances of making it were still slim.

Michael was visiting the next time the nurse entered my room with the afternoon doses of chemo. He watched as she brought a bag of thick, dark blue, inklike fluid over to my bed. She carried it like a ceremonial offering, holding the bag up at face level and wearing protective gloves and a gown. A face mask was hanging loosely around her neck. Suspenseful silence filled the room. After hooking up the chemo, the nurse removed her disposable protective gown, and wrapping the gloves and face mask in the gown, she deposited them in a special container. Standing at the foot of my bed, Michael watched the dark blue drops as they proceeded down the line on their way to my heart. Although I forced a smile, as always I was feeling apprehensive, as if I were about to be poisoned. Tears came to my eyes. My body seemed heavier at times like these, and I would sink deeper into the sheets. Earlier in my treatments I would think of these sensations of weight and being drawn down as defeating and I would try to fight them, but I learned to trust them and to just experience the fall. The bed, Mother Earth, my family and friends, my teacher, were always there to help support the weight that was too heavy for this suddenly old man.

Mike was solemn. Here lay his brother, the health nut, being assaulted by toxic chemicals administered directly into his heart. Mike used to enjoy poking fun at me because of my vegetarianism and health habits, but on this day he was filled with compassion. "Jesus, Jimmy," he said in a low voice while shaking his head, "no wonder you lose your hair."

Although he often thought that my affinity with the Buddha's teaching was a little far-out, he placed his hand gently on my leg and said, "Jim, don't think of this stuff as poison or toxic waste. Think of those drops as little blue buddhas coming to help heal you."

I found his advice very helpful and did indeed use that metaphor to put my mind at ease many times. I could see the helplessness in his face. He then said something that I was to hear often over the next several months. "Jim," he said, "if I could take a turn in that bed for a while, you know, to give you a break, I'd take a few shifts for you."

As I looked up at his despondent face, there was no doubt in my mind that he meant it. My family, Zen teacher, and friends, when seeing me at my worst would also sit looking compassionately, wishing that they, too, could help share the burden. Indeed they were. The load always seemed lighter when visiting loved ones would sit with me in support.

The next morning it was Margaret's turn to share in the ceremony. I looked over at her as she watched the toxic drugs being administered to her already enfeebled husband. I could see the deep worry and fear on her face. I, too, was worried about the effects the drug would have on an already diminished body.

"Margaret," I said, "I don't ever want you to forget how much I really appreciate your love and support. Promise me, Margaret, that if I don't get through this, you'll tell our children often how much their father loved them. One of the most important things in the world to me is that they don't ever forget how much I love them. Margaret, I don't know if I remember my youth all that well. Do you think they'll remember me when they grow older?"

Margaret tried to reassure me that I was going to be one of those who made it. Often I would hear my mother or my siblings trying to comfort me, saying, "Don't worry, Jim, you'll make it." Or, "You know, Jim, I really know in my heart that you are going to pull through this."

I had no such conviction, nor did I want it. It wasn't real. Many of the other patients I met were being told not to worry and that they were "definitely going to make it" by loved ones just before they died. Death was all around me and I didn't want to ignore it. I felt as though I had made peace with the inevitable dropping off of my body and mind and was reconciled to the knowledge that I was going to die. Perhaps it would not come in the next week, perhaps not in the next month, perhaps not for a while, but it was a realization that came at a price, and I wasn't willing to let go of this wisdom so hard to gain.

This does not mean that I was not choosing life. On the contrary, I was still on a tightrope, trying to balance between denial of the possibility of death and falling into an apathetic, defeatist attitude. Each moment demanded attention to the present. Meanwhile, I tried not to lose sight of my long-term goal of returning to a healthy and more normal lifestyle.

One encountered the extremes of both denial and defeat in the halls and in the rooms on that seventh floor at St. Michael's Hospital. A woman across the hall told her doctors that if her test turned out to be positive and she did in fact have "C," as she referred to it, she did not want to be told. She did have advanced cancer, which her family, nurses, and even other patients knew about. But she did not. At least she never spoke to her family or anyone else about it. I still can't figure out why she thought she was in the hospital, but I'm sure she did her best not to think about it.

Others pleaded with death to take them because they felt they would never be able to deal with the suffering involved in the treatments. I was somewhere in the middle, and when I did lose my footing, I was usually quick to recognize the warning signs, or was quickly reminded by one of my friends or my teacher, and went to work immediately to regain composure and balance. Then carefully, moment by moment, breath after breath, I carried on.

I began to get a reputation for being positive and would often be encouraged by the nurses to visit other patients and their families. I was told that it was heartening for others to see me so "upbeat" and that my visits would help cheer them. One woman who had heard of my ordeal asked me to visit her sister who had cancer and was suffering terribly. I felt grateful to have an opportunity to help her and others.

The woman I visited was very depressed. Her prognosis was not good and she knew she was not responding well to the chemo. When I visited her I told her that the odds the doctors gave her were far better than those I had been given when I was first diagnosed, so not to lose hope. Then I recounted a little of my ordeal in ICU, hoping not to say anything that would frighten her or her family who were visiting. I wanted to give her and her guests enough information to know that it was possible to get through some very trying times. Then, standing in a boxerlike stance I kidded with them, saying that I was not yet ready for the pine box. "Not tonight anyway," I said. I then asked the woman, "Did you order breakfast for tomorrow?"

"Oh yes," she replied. We were both fond of the yogurt and prunes they served in the morning.

"Well, then," I said, "for now, let's look forward to breakfast. You have a peaceful night."

Before I left she asked me some questions about diarrhea and the swelling I had on my hands and feet, as she too was quite swollen in those areas. I told her about the swelling and then said, "For me, if I'm not messing with diarrhea, I seem to be struggling with constipation, and this complicates things for me spiritually." Taking some pleasure in their puzzled looks for a moment, I said, "Well, you see, I'm a Buddhist, and Buddhists are supposed to practice the Middle Way." When I left, they were all laughing.

My health actually seemed to improve for the next few days, and I was beginning to believe that this second round of treatment was indeed going to be easier than the first. I had done quite well with the chemo and was now waiting for my counts to drop. About a week after the chemo had begun, the resident doctor on call was visiting and I asked him how long I could expect to keep feeling so well. He reiterated to my mother, Margaret, and me that it was not uncommon to see patients do much better the second time around. He felt that the body did a better job adjusting to the chemo in subsequent treatments and thus responded in a less severe manner.

I was encouraged to hear this, but when I recounted it to my hematologist he warned me that I had not yet begun to experience the side effects of the chemo and that it could often take longer than a week for the effects to begin. He then said, "You know, Jim, experiencing chemotherapy treatments is kind of like getting hit by a truck. It is usually better the second time around—it's like the difference between getting hit by a five-ton truck instead of a ten-ton truck—but you're still going to feel like you've been hit by a truck. So prepare yourself. We hit you pretty hard this time." My mom, Margaret, and I found it quite humorous to hear it put that way, but we appreciated the warning.

He was definitely right. Over the next week or so my health deteriorated drastically. Ian, Ross, and Randy would take turns visiting every day, as they had all along. It was not unusual for me to wake up and find one of them sitting quietly in my room doing zazen. Once I was awake they would offer to read to me or ask if I preferred to visit or just continue resting. Many times after asking one of them to read me a Zen Buddhist text I would end up dozing off. Sensei often said that Zen was to be practiced and experienced, not pondered over. So when I'd wake up I would joke with the guys that I was really off in a deep state of concentration, directly experiencing the truth, while they were merely reading about it.

Food was becoming a real problem for me. When my counts were low I was put on a low-microbial diet, which meant no fresh fruit or vegetables, no unprocessed cheese, no yogurt or nuts, and many other restrictions. Often for lunch I would be served processed cheese on white bread. When Sunyana-sensei heard that being a vegetarian complicated matters for me considerably, she asked the sangha to orchestrate a food plan. Everyone worked hard to make meals that could be warmed in the microwave at the hospital. Many of our members prepared special foods according to my nutritionist's instructions. I received deliveries of twice-baked potatoes and great vegetarian soups. Whenever there was a retreat, the head cook put aside food for me, and Ian, Ross, or Randy would leave the retreat once or twice each day—something not usually permitted—and visit me, bringing with them some fine fare. This made things much easier. I still feel grateful for all the tasty and nourishing food I received from my many friends during those turbulent months.

Ian, Ross, and Randy always checked with me before signing up to attend a sesshin, knowing that I would see them less for that period, especially if the retreat was at the center in Vermont, in which case I would not see them at all. I always encouraged them to go. "There will always be reasons to miss sesshin, but unless it is a real emergency, we must respond to an even deeper call not to miss sesshin," I told them. When I was unconscious in ICU I had clearly heard a cry for help from suffering beings. Ever since then

I have felt deeply that the call to spiritual practice does not stem only from our own needs but is also a response to the natural human desire to help others. Our interconnectedness with all beings is the foundation of spiritual effort.

The next few days were a constant downward spiral. The sores in my mouth returned and I again lost all sense of taste. I developed throat infections and excruciating headaches and earaches. My cough was worse and I feared that I would develop pneumonia and again be facing the respirator and muscle atrophy. I was strong enough to be walking every day and did not want to fall behind and have to rely on the wheelchair again. So I made it a point, no matter how sick I felt, to get out of bed and walk around the room several times a day. Then, standing facing the altar, I would offer a bow of gratitude. I had strategically placed my Kannon altar so that when returning from the toilet or my short walk I would naturally face it before getting into bed again. I did this to remind myself to offer a gassho for those chanting on my behalf, a bow of gratitude for the help I had received from the sangha and all my friends and family. I also offered a bow of thanks because I knew that as each day passed it would never have to be lived again. I felt grateful for having had the opportunity to expiate this karma while I had a human body, a spiritual practice, and the loving support of family and friends. Karmic debts—like money owed—grow the longer they are kept. So I knew I was better off experiencing this suffering now than deferring it to the future. I was no hero and many times passed the altar without bowing or having taken the Three Refuges three times a day, as I had planned. However, most days I was able to do this and to include some chanting and some informal zazen.

Eating became a big challenge once more. At times even water was too much for my infected throat. My blood levels had dropped considerably, and once again, confined to isolation, I began to chart my red and white blood counts, platelets, and daily temperature. Then I waited for the long days to pass.

Within the week my counts hit bottom and I was given blood products again. The doctors had two major concerns: my body did not seem to want to hold the platelets (my platelet counts would drop very soon after the new products had been administered), and I had developed an infection that might necessitate the removal of my Hickman line. I was very discouraged to hear this, as it meant that I would have to have another one inserted when my platelets and white blood cell counts were high enough. In the meantime, they would have to administer blood products through intravenous needles in my arm. I already received several needles and blood tests each day. My arms and buttocks were bruised and tired from the numerous punctures.

That same night, the nurses told me that there was a delay in getting the platelets they had ordered that morning. Normal platelet count is about 150. Eight to ten days after the chemo began my counts would start to drop. When the counts fell to below 20 they would give me a pint of platelets, and usually my counts would go up to about 38 or 40. But on this night my counts were 14 and falling, and as my blood type was the rare AB negative, they were having trouble finding the product I so critically needed. A platelet count this low posed a risk of internal bleeding.

As the evening wore on my platelets continued to drop. I could tell it was becoming serious. I felt exhausted, my nose began to bleed, and I was coughing up blood. Soon the rigors began, and I said to Margaret, "You know, I really think this could be it. I feel awful, and I have no strength this time, no fight at all." Shaking my head I said, "Really, Margaret, I have nothing left." I felt completely drained.

The nurses continued to check my counts regularly that evening and throughout the night. The platelet counts dropped below 10, then down to 4. After that they no longer told us what the counts were but just said that the platelets they had ordered were on the way. Margaret spent the night in a chair in my room again. I was conscious and awake most of the night and the rigors seemed far worse than in the past. It was a "socks on, socks off" night. The fevers and chills came in relentless waves that made rest impossible for either of us.

As the night wore on, Margaret became increasing alarmed. She asked about the delay in getting the platelets and was told again that they should be arriving soon. When she returned to my room and found me with raised eyebrows and an anxious look, she simply said, "The check's in the mail."

The doctor on call came to see me and said that my condition was becoming critical and they were going to have to administer some platelets even though they were not the type I needed. The doctor warned us, saying, "The rigors will definitely be worse than what you have faced in the past and there will be a ten percent chance that this will complicate things with the bone marrow transplant. But, Jim, we have to make a call here to get you through this until we can find the product we need." The incompatible platelets were administered.

The rigors got much worse, and the night seemed to last forever. Margaret patiently removed my blankets and socks and wiped me down with cold cloths, then covered me up again when the chills began. My condition deteriorated rapidly. I was bleeding from my nose, mouth, throat, and rectum. The bleeding eventually lessened, but the rigors continued on through the night.

The next day, just before noon, the compatible single-donor platelets arrived. Within an hour after receiving them I felt much better. What gratitude I felt for the stranger who had donated this product that saved my life!

Margaret and I both looked up at an emptying bag of platelets, a thick, yellow substance I could not go without. "Thank you, my friend," I said aloud and received a smile from the nurse and my exhausted wife.

I remembered the times I had heard requests for blood from the Red Cross. Here I had been in serious condition because blood products were not available. I was glad that I had been a regular donor, and from that day on each time the life-giving fluids were brought into my room I would place my hands in gassho and do a bow of thanks to my donors, without whom I simply would not have survived. I immediately asked if I could give blood in the future—I wanted to repay the favor someday—but was told that, after all these treatments, I would never again be accepted as a donor. Now whenever people ask me if there is anything they can do to help, I reply, "Yes, there is—*give blood.*"

6

THE FAITH
TO DOUBT

It is proper to doubt. Do not be led by holy scriptures,
or by mere logic or inference, or by appearances,
or by the authority of religious teachers.
But when you realize that something
is unwholesome and bad for you, give it up.
And when you realize that something
is wholesome and good for you, do it.

—SHAKYAMUNI BUDDHA

IN THE HOSPITAL I often heard parents, siblings, grandparents,
and spouses of the sick praying for their loved ones to be well.
One family I met was dealing not only with a person slightly older
than I who had leukemia but with the patient's seriously ill grand-
daughter as well. She had cancer of the liver and was across the
street in Sick Children's Hospital waiting for a transplant. When
they returned from mass or from the hospital chapel, I often heard
one of them trying to convince the others that God would surely
answer their prayers. One day the grandmother of the sick child
reassured her daughter, the child's mother, that she knew in her

heart that "God was listening this morning." The young girl died before the end of the week.

The night after I received the single-donor platelets, an elderly woman fell as she was trying to go to the washroom. She broke her pelvis, and her cries could be heard echoing off the empty hallway walls as they rushed her to emergency. "Oh God, help me! Please, God, help me!"

I remembered the elderly man who had been my roommate a week or so earlier. Every night, he called out to God. He was embittered and angry with the nurses, his wife, and his family who visited during the day. At night, when he felt most alone, he whispered to God, "Please don't let me die. Oh, God, please don't let me die." It did not seem to matter to him how miserable his life was as long as he didn't have to face death. I wondered why he did not long for peace. His pleas and cravings for existence helped me understand why some beings choose to be reborn regardless of which realm they find themselves in.

One young man who had been my roommate for about a week before I was confined to isolation was dying of AIDS, though he had not told me this. Leukemia was his AIDS-confirming illness. He had known he was HIV-positive for some time, but the tests for leukemia revealed that he had AIDS as well. We spoke often and shared many afternoons chatting and offering each other support. He could see by my altar that I was a Buddhist. "Jim," he once said to me, "you seem to be very accepting of your illness, almost as if it were some sort of spiritual practice."

For me illness was indeed a spiritual practice, as it still is, as is good health. How can we separate our life from our spiritual practice? Spiritual practice does not begin or end with sitting in meditation, chanting, or saying a prayer. Our life is our spiritual practice, our prayer. Those who feel that offering up a prayer from time to time, or at the time of their death, will have sufficient saving grace to compensate for whatever pain they have caused others may be in for a rude awakening.

The day before he left to go home, my ex-roommate entered my room and, looking bewildered, told me that he had AIDS. "I don't know why God has dealt me these cards," he said. "I contracted HIV ten years ago—it was my very first sexual experience. I was eighteen years old, and now . . . with my having AIDS and leukemia too . . . well?" He shrugged his shoulders, turned his palms up, and stood with a blank stare as if frozen in time. How I wished we had started that conversation days earlier. I wanted to reach out to him, to tell him something about the law of causation and how it had helped me understand and deal with my own suffering. But there was nothing I could do. His mother was waiting in the hall. He was leaving, and I wasn't going anywhere.

"It was great rooming with you, Jim," he said. "Keep your chin up. I'm sure I'll be seeing you around."

"I hope not," came my reply.

We both smiled. He knew that I was going to be in the hospital for the next four or five weeks, and if I did see him, it would be because his failing health brought him back. Unfortunately, it was not long before I was again asking about my friend across the hall. Since I was in isolation and he had an infection, we could not visit each other, but every so often he stood in the hall, opened my door, and offered a quick thumbs up and a kind smile of encouragement to his gaunt friend under the sheets.

I have heard many patients ask the question, "Why does God allow me to suffer so?" Their spirits were defeated, their faith shaken, and their hearts longed for peace.

On a talk show I saw from my hospital bed, I heard TV celebrities who had cancer speak about how, although they couldn't understand "why" God gave them this illness, they never doubted his love. Moreover, their faith was not compromised by their affliction. It is admirable to have such faith, but it still does not answer the fundamental question of suffering.

A picture I had seen on television from the days of the drought in Ethiopia came to mind: a field strewn with bodies and a young child desperately trying to suckle her dead mother's dried-up breast. Not knowing about the law of causation at that time, I watched in horror and wondered why a compassionate God would allow people to suffer so.

I remembered reading what C. S. Lewis had said as he watched his wife dying from cancer. "If even I would take away this suffering, take it on myself, why won't God?"

The nightly news told of genocide in Rwanda, chaos in India, riots in Ireland, violence in homes in North America, and anguish in so many places in the world. People were suffering at the hands of other humans. I felt as if I were drowning in a sea of suffering.

A few days passed and I went through the usual ups and downs with severe headaches and earaches while trying to "practice in the midst of activity." At times I was unable to meditate or chant and felt I wasn't doing enough. At other times I accepted that I was doing my best by simply taking the Three Refuges and reciting the four vows while holding my hands in gassho. I reminded myself that just lying in bed mindfully, weak and nauseated, was my spiritual practice.

Margaret returned home to be with the children. Although our children were doing a great job of looking after themselves, I always urged her to be sure to spend enough time with them, since I had many other visitors. A few days after she arrived home, Margaret called to tell me that Raymond, our youngest, had been rushed to the hospital to have his appendix removed.

I called him at the hospital to give him my love and some encouraging words. He was afraid of surgery, and nothing I said seemed to put his mind at ease. Within an hour Margaret called again. I could hear the shakiness in her voice. "Jim, I don't know how I'm going to tell you this." She hesitated, "Raymond's not breathing. He had an allergic reaction to the anesthetic and they will have to keep him on a respirator. The doctor is on the phone now calling the specialists to find out something about his enzymes. I don't know how serious it is. The doctors are very concerned." She then broke down and cried.

Moments later a nurse who was taking blood from my line told me that the woman I had visited, the one with the swollen hands and feet, had died.

Pain, suffering, sickness, and death were all around me. There did not seem to be anywhere they had not touched. There did not seem to be any being who was not suffering. The world was a dim place that night. For a short time I wondered why I had decided to go ahead with the treatments and suffer so, since in the end I would just have to face sickness, old age, and death. I wanted to escape. But there was nowhere to turn.

My first thoughts were to leave the hospital to visit my frightened son. I knew how important it was for me to stay in isolation, but I no longer cared. I was engulfed in a sea of confusion, pain, suffering, and death. There was no deep peace to save me from falling. Not this time. I wanted to leave to be at his side.

My family, none of whom were in town that night, suspected I would react in this way and called to see if one of my friends could visit me. But it was the night of a special sangha dinner, and Ian, Ross, and Randy were there at a restaurant far from the hospital. Just then my dear friend Schoel called and asked if I wanted a visitor. I began to tell him about Raymond.

"Jim," he said, "actually I'm about ten feet from your room at the nursing station. You won't believe this, but my car broke down a few minutes ago, literally in front of the hospital. I didn't want you to feel obliged to see me, so I thought I'd call and check first." Schoel came in and stayed to help me deal with my loneliness. A few hours later, Randy showed up—my family had tracked him down at the restaurant. Even though I was comforted by the warmth of their support, my heart was still torn. I felt as if I were ten thousand miles away from my ailing son.

I didn't know whether or not Raymond was dying and I longed to be at his side. Nor did I have any idea of how long I was going to live, and I didn't want to miss this time to be with him. I wanted him to have memories of support from his father as he grew older.

I was coughing a great deal. The coughing made the headaches and earaches almost unbearable and the turmoil in my mind seemed insurmountable. A thousand thoughts about karma and suffering arose and remained with me long after Schoel and Randy had gone.

The room was quiet, and never before in my life had I felt so alone. For the only time I can remember, I became angry with my illness. It had stolen my life from me, and I accepted that, but I was not about to easily give up my responsibilities as a father to my children in their time of need, not as long as there was breath in my nostrils. It just didn't seem fair to my children. They had suffered enough because of my illness and we were still only in the beginning stages. Why should they have to go through difficult times in their lives without my support? Was it their karma? Was it my karma? Ray's karma?

I knew that looking into these questions intellectually was not the answer. The conceptual mind is so limited. I had been there a thousand times before. Abandoning myself to thoughts would stir up endless other thoughts.

In the early eighties, soon after I had begun to practice Zen, I had tried to look at spiritual matters through the thinking mind. It was around that time that a friend of mine had died of bone cancer. He was a very compassionate and caring individual—to my knowledge he had never hurt anyone in his life—and I could not figure out the "why" of his suffering. At the time of his death, my mind filled with a thousand questions. It demanded answers. I challenged the teachings I held to be most sacred. I questioned the whole idea of karma and rebirth. I doubted my practice, life, Buddhism, everything I had learned and believed to be true. I was like a wild animal caught in a trap trying frantically to escape. I could not believe that suffering was meaningless, nor could I accept that it was the will of a benevolent God. Karma was the answer that kept coming up. Eventually, I realized that it was impossible to try to understand the Infinite with the finite mind. As Zen master Tokusan once said, "Even if one gains all the essential knowledge in the world, it is like throwing a drop of water into a deep ravine."

Now, on this night in the hospital, I began my meditation by looking directly into Mind. I sat quietly with an open heart, questioning, *Who am I? What am I?* Sitting still, I began by looking into the mind of confusion.

Confusing thoughts are confusing thoughts . . .

Doubt and bewilderment, only doubt and bewilderment . . .

The formations of consciousness, just formations . . .

When I let go of these, who or what am I? What is it that is aware at this moment?

My questioning deepened and engulfed me. Everywhere I looked there was darkness. In this darkness I pushed on and on until I came to a point where I could go no further. *Who am I? What am I?* A thousand crystal chambers shattered and fell. *All things are right, just as they are!* The universe was indeed unfolding as it should. We reap what we sow; for every cause there is an effect.

I remembered those months of challenging the teachings with every fiber of my being, and I was glad that I had done so years ago. I had learned in my bones the truth of the law of causation.

A feeling of gratitude enveloped me. Like the wonder one feels seeing a blade of grass growing through pavement, I was awed to find gratitude making its way into such a dark place on that challenging night. The work I had done in the past, my years of training in Zen, resurfaced when I needed it most.

How can one feel gratitude in the face of a ravaging illness? I was grateful for my suffering in the sense that I knew that karma was being expiated with each passing moment. I was grateful for an understanding of what a difference the Buddha's teachings had made in my dealing with this illness. I was grateful to have had the opportunity to have practiced for years *before* becoming ill.

Whenever I face great doubt, I remind myself that this doubt itself can lead to new insight and a deeper appreciation of who and what I am. Doubt is a call to deepen our understanding. If we look directly into the source of our confusion—into our own Mind—we will emerge changed by the experience.

Later that night a nurse came in to tell me they had an emergency call for me. It was late, and no calls are permitted into the hospital after ten o'clock, but the nurses transferred the call to my room from their line. They knew about Raymond's condition.

"Raymond's okay," Margaret's faint and tired voice came through the receiver. "He's resting now and you'll be able to speak with him in the morning. His body was able to deal with the drug reaction eventually. The doctors said he's going to be fine . . . think you'll be able to get some rest tonight?"

"Yeah," I replied. "I'm fine really, just so relieved to hear that Ray's okay. Don't worry about me. You try and get some rest. Talk to you tomorrow."

The next morning for the first time since being readmitted I slept well. When the breakfast tray came I just turned over and went back to sleep. I was awakened by the insistent ringing of the telephone.

A frail voice came over the receiver, "Hi, Dad, it's me, Raymond. I'm OK."

"Raymond?!"

"I'm hooked up to an intravenous pump, too, Dad." I could tell by his voice that he was still under sedation and very groggy.

"Is your pump like mine?" I asked.

"Yeah, it's the same. What's your pump set at, Dad?"

"Mine's set at seventy-five, what's yours at?"

"Hey, mine's set at seventy-five too."

Although I didn't let him know it, I was crying. It was so wonderful to hear his sweet voice and to hear him say that he was okay.

Raymond described his battle scar and told me he remembered not being able to breathe.

"Dad, I couldn't understand why they wouldn't let me wake up. I kept trying to wake up and they kept putting me back to sleep. Now I know that I have pseudocholinesterase deficiency, and I can spell it too." Then he spelled the word that I still have trouble pronouncing.

No sooner had I hung up the phone than it rang again. It was the nurse from the bone marrow transplant unit at Princess Margaret Hospital. "Mr. Bedard," she said, "this is the call you've been waiting for. You have two potential donors among your siblings: your brother John and your sister Shirley-Anne. They're both good matches. Good luck if you decide to go ahead with the transplant." She explained that there are six main categories in which tests are done. If the blood was compatible in four or five out of the six categories a transplant would be possible. Both John and Shirley-Anne were six out of six matches. Great news indeed!

Soon I was on the phone telling everyone the exciting news. First I called John and Shirley-Anne. They were so happy, you'd have thought they had won an Oscar.

When we had originally discussed the transplant I had been under the impression that the donor's pelvic bone would need to be punctured six to eight times to collect the spongy tissue. My hematologist, however, had since enlightened me on the subject and I had the "pleasure" of informing my potential donors of the error.

When I spoke to John and Shirley-Anne I began my conversation with, "Remember how I told you that they would have to put you to sleep and puncture the pelvis with a thick threaded needle six or eight times? Well, I was a little off on the number of punctures. My doctor tells me that it's really about one hundred and fifty times."

At this we all had a good laugh. They teased me, saying that my original false presentation was intentional to get their commitment. I agreed that "of course" it was so. After the laughter died down I continued, "Are you really sure you want to do this?" Even knowing that the donor had to undergo surgery and tolerate the pain of all those bone marrow aspirations, it didn't seem to matter to them at all. Both John and Shirley-Anne reassured me that even if they had to give up a limb, they weren't backing out. Although one is asleep for the operation, I could barely imagine the pain the donor would experience once awake. Just one puncture of the pelvic bone left me feeling very sore. But they knew as well as I did that without their commitment my chances of beating the disease were negligible.

The doctors said that we would have to do further testing to see who would be the better match. However, probably they would go with the same-sex donor. Women who have male children develop antibodies against the "y" chromosome. My sister was the mother of male children and this could cause more complications for me with graft-versus-host disease.

What a relief! As I told everyone the good news, I broke down and cried. I was actually beginning to feel that I had a chance of being cured. Finding a compatible donor was such an important step on the long road to recovery.

I had met others who were waiting to see if they could find a match in the public pool. That was a harrowing ordeal. I spent one evening with three women who were all waiting for dates for bone marrow transplants. One of the women had just learned that a match had been found in the public pool. The other two women were waiting, hoping that some day, before it was too late, they too would get a phone call. Neither had a match in the family.

Within the next week my counts again began to rise and my mouth could once more tolerate food. I called the Zen Centre, as I knew that Sunyana-sensei and Randy were planning on visiting me that day, and asked them to bring me a spinach and potato roti.[1]

When the door to my room opened, a procession entered. I could scarcely contain my joy: Sensei was in the lead, with Randy following and holding up the roti like a precious offering. They entered and greeted me with beaming faces. I winked at Ian, who was also visiting, and said to him, "Don't you say a word."

I hadn't eaten for more than a week and my mouth was not quite ready for food that needed chewing, but even so, my sense of taste had returned. Although the eating was somewhat painful, I thoroughly enjoyed every bite. My visitors were surprised to see how well I was doing—and so was I. It seemed amazing that only twelve hours earlier I was suffering greatly with a racking cough and ear and head pain. These quick changes in my health taught me to just go along for the ride, to experience the highs and the lows without holding fast to either extreme. One never knew how the next few hours were going to be, let alone the next day or the next week. No matter how bad things became I would remind myself, *Who knows, perhaps by this afternoon or this evening, I'll be up walking and eating again.*

When I had eaten about half the roti, I let the cat out of the bag. I told them that Ian had already shown up with a roti and I was enjoying my *second* one in a matter of an hour. For someone who had not eaten for days and had a shrunken stomach, I was managing the indulgence just fine. We all had a good chuckle, and although I could not finish the second roti, I soon felt strength returning to my body from the much-appreciated nourishment.

My hematologist visited and told me that my counts had begun to climb. I knew this meant the worst was over for the time being. He also told me that the infection they suspected was coming from my central venous catheter had cleared up and the catheter would not have to be removed. We took out the calendar and marked the date of my meeting with the bone marrow transplant team at Princess Margaret Hospital. I was hoping to get scheduled early and get it over with before the holiday season. It was still early in November, and I secretly wondered if I would ever again spend Christmas with my family.

Before my hematologist left I asked him for permission to leave the hospital at the end of the week to attend a Jukai ceremony at our center in Toronto.[2] I would probably be out of isolation by the week's end but knew that catching a cold or flu could be very dangerous. One man from my floor had caught a cold that led to pneumonia and eventually his death; I was lying in the bed he once occupied. I also knew, as did my doctor, that I might never get another chance to attend Jukai again. He said that I could go as long as there would be no hugging or shaking of hands with others. I agreed.

Later that week Mike picked me up on a cold morning in early November to take me to the Zen Centre. I was soon sitting with my hands palm-to-palm taking the precepts. My heart was full when I saw the center again and sat with Sensei and the sangha, all of whom had helped me so much.

After the ceremony I spoke to Sunyana-sensei in private. She asked me if I thought I would have the energy to give a talk to the sangha. I agreed and told Sensei that my experiences while in ICU had so confirmed my faith in the dharma that I'd be happy to share what I had seen while I had the chance.

We planned my dharma talk for November 15, when I would be out of the hospital. Little did we know that I would be arriving at the center that day exhausted from having spent more than five hours with the medical team at the transplant unit going over all the details of the procedure, the many possible side effects, and my chances of survival.

I began my talk with, "If I sound tired and weak tonight, it is simply because I *am* very tired and very weak, but let me begin with a saying from ancient China. . . ."

7

VISITING OTHER REALMS

Now when the death-point . . . dawns upon me,
I will give up the preoccupation of the all-desiring
  mind . . .
And transmigrate into the birthless space of inner
  awareness;
About to lose this created body of flesh and blood,
I will realize it to be impermanent illusion!

— THE TIBETAN BOOK OF THE DEAD

I ARRIVED AT THE ZEN CENTRE exhausted. Margaret and I had met with several doctors from the transplant team and spent more than five hours discussing possible dangers and my chances for survival. Most discouraging for me was to hear that I would have to return to St. Michael's Hospital for a third round of chemotherapy and four or five weeks of isolation whether or not I went ahead with the transplant. Furthermore, if I did decide to have the transplant, I would have to undergo additional treatments at Princess Margaret Hospital (PMH).

The doctors at PMH had been frank in their presentation: the next round of chemotherapy would be similar to the round I had just gone through. The first three treatments were serious assaults on the blood and bone marrow. However, the fourth treatment, immediately before the transplant, would include radiation and be the most severe yet. It was designed to completely kill the marrow in an attempt to rid the body of all leukemia cells and make room for the new marrow to engraft.

There were many side effects I might experience: serious nausea, vomiting, loss of appetite, mouth sores, jaundice, abdominal pain, confusion, pneumonia, diarrhea, fatigue; damage to the digestive tract, lungs, liver, testes, and stomach; swollen neck glands; and many other risks, including possible death. I was also told that I would be sterile after the radiation and the heavier doses of chemotherapy, that my bones would be far more brittle than the normal person's, and that my energy level and everyday health would probably never return to normal. It was as if they had given me a choice between doors number one and number two and I had been hoping all along that there would be a door number three. There was not. Returning to the vibrant, healthy life I had been used to was not an option. Someone whom I had loved very dearly had died.

The doctors tried to encourage me, saying that the transplant would give me the best overall odds to survive the disease. "We did a survey last year and about ninety percent of those we interviewed said they were glad they had gone ahead with the transplant. Most felt a new appreciation for life and a sense of confidence that they were better prepared to face life's many challenges."

"Doc," I asked, "did you call only the ones who survived the transplant and the treatments?"

". . . That's an interesting point, Mr. Bedard," the doctor responded.

Knowing that it was going to be tougher than anything I had experienced to date, I left the meeting disappointed and discouraged. The doctors had told me that there was a 25 percent chance that I was already cured of the disease, but unfortunately there was no way to know if this was so. If I waited to find out whether I would relapse, by the time the leukemia was advanced enough to be detected, it would probably be too late to do anything about it. AML leukemia is an acute type and a fast mover. If I relapsed, it would be even more difficult to make it to a second remission, which would significantly decrease my chances of having a successful transplant.

It was clear that I was facing considerable suffering, with a 10 percent chance that I would die before leaving the hospital and only a 50 percent chance of surviving after months of very trying times. The percentages of survival were very confusing and it was hard for me to be excited about my options. At one point I stopped the doctor and asked him, "If I die, will I be 50 percent or 60 percent dead?" He looked uncomfortable. "If I die," I reassured him, "I'm sure I'll be 100 percent dead."

Despite the necessity, the doctors were hesitant to talk in terms of percentages, as it often got them in trouble. They said that one person who had been told his chances of survival were about 75 percent became livid when he learned that he was not going to make it and that he had just a few weeks to live.

The doctor told me, "You're right about percentages. They can be very misleading, but they can help patients considering a transplant make decisions. I'm sure you're aware that you are the most important person on our team and we would not even consider booking you until you are completely sure you want to go ahead with this. It's not easy on us when we lose someone early in the transplant process knowing that the person might have survived a year or more without it. You're not the healthy young forty-year-old you were six months ago, and as you know, we'll have to hit you much harder than anything you've experienced to date. So give it a lot of thought."

That afternoon Margaret and I watched videos on transplant procedures, met the primary-care nurses, and had a tour of the Bone Marrow Transplant Unit at Princess Margaret Hospital. It was an intense time for us. Once I was better informed, I was no longer sure that I wanted to go ahead with the transplant. At a time when I wished to be focused and confident—just before giving a dharma talk—I was confused, discouraged, and afraid.

Once I arrived at the center, the few rounds of meditation before the talk gave me the time I needed to focus my mind and let go of the turbulence. I began:

> There is a saying from ancient China that "if one preaches a false teaching his eyebrows will fall out." I thought this would be an ideal time for me to give a talk, because should I lose the little bit of eyebrow I have left, I can always blame the chemo.

With this there was laughter, and a feeling of ease spread through the room, helping me relax into the talk.

There was so much I wanted to share with the sangha. While I was in ICU and unaware of my body for days on end, the Buddhist teachings of karma, the interconnectedness of all things, and the existence of other realms were confirmed to me on a profound level. Even though I was unconscious, drugged, or seemingly asleep, rest was impossible. The noise of the mind was turned off—the senses did not respond in the normal way—but my mind did not disappear. I encountered dream states, deeper states of consciousness, and even out-of-body experiences.

One time, after I had been out of ICU and back in my room for several weeks, I met a fellow who lived near me. His wife had just been diagnosed with AML leukemia, and he was extremely upset. My brother brought him in to meet me, knowing that he would be encouraged to see how well I was after my close brush with death. We spoke briefly and he left. I did not get a chance to meet his wife, since she was on a respirator and I was just out of isolation. That night I focused on her as best I could while taking the Three Refuges and chanting the *Prajña Paramita*. Then I went to sleep. It had been a long time since I slept well, but that night I slept very deeply. Or at least my body did.

Soon after I fell asleep, I became aware of the woman whose husband I had briefly met, calling out for help. She thought she was dying and was terribly frightened. I took her hand and we floated above the hospital. Looking down at the roof and the pattern of the cars in the parking lot, I smiled and reassured her that she was going to be okay. After a while we traveled to other parts of Toronto and she became less afraid. When she was feeling more comfortable, she smiled and said, "I have to go now." Then I lost connection with her.

Soon I found myself in my old hometown trying to contact my parents. By then I was no longer aware that I was out of my body, or dreaming, and I was lost. I could not find out how to get back to the hospital or how to get home. I recognized my parents' neighborhood but still could not figure out how to get to their house. I realized that I really should not have been out of the hospital.

This has got to be a dream! I thought. I tried to wake myself several times, but I could not. (Normally, whenever I realize I am dreaming, it is very difficult *not* to wake up immediately.) Bending down I smelled the grass, then, turning my head, I looked carefully at the stars and trees. I noticed a large redbrick building that seemed out of place. It had not been there when I grew up in that neighborhood. I walked behind the building and saw a pile of planks used for construction. Beside the planks was a stack of cement blocks. *Where the hell am I? I don't remember this building. Am I dreaming? I've never had a dream like this before,* I thought. *But this has to be a dream. Unless . . . Wait! Perhaps I've died and that's how I came to meet that woman earlier.*

Again I tried to wake myself up, but I could not. I began hovering over the town trying to feel out my family and friends. I needed confirmation of my death and thought I might be able to get in touch with my body and find a coffin or hospital bed surrounded by my loved ones. After searching for a time I recognized the hospital and the parking lot I had seen earlier.

Wham! Startled, I sat up in bed in my hospital room, sweating and wide awake. *What the hell was that all about? It was so real. The smelling of the grass and that walk behind the redbrick building were as real as this lying here. Well, I thought, at least I'm still alive for another night. At least I think I am.*

Even though I felt very weak, I got out of bed and peered down at the parking lot to check what I thought I had seen. I had not looked out my window earlier that evening. Now I could see that the cars were in exactly the same pattern that I had seen in my "dream."

The next day I was told that the woman had died that night. I tried to pass it off, feeling that perhaps it was no more than a coincidence. Yet, I could not readily dismiss what I had seen and felt.

The fact that I had somehow become aware of the pattern of cars in the hospital parking lot was haunting, but I tried not to dwell on it. A couple of months later, I was in North Bay for a visit and drove by the old neighborhood where, on that fall evening in my "dream," I had bent down and smelled the grass. To my surprise a large redbrick building had been constructed on a vacant lot since I had grown up there. *Now that's interesting,* I thought. I took a minute to drive around the back and found a pile of planks and a stack of cement blocks, exactly as I had seen them on that night.

That's amazing, I thought, *how could I possibly have known about this place?* Another weird coincidence? Perhaps. Still, what I had seen and felt on that day was as real to me as the nausea, pain, and debility I also experienced.

I also told the sangha about the time in ICU when I was expected to live for only a few more hours. That day, I entered a state between life and death, as my mind was drawn further and further away from my body. I gradually became aware of a boundless expanse of light, an endless moonlight, soothing and comforting. There was no sense of self or having a body. I had disappeared into limitless, birthless space. For what seemed to be an eternity, I rested in a place I had never really left.

Suddenly I became aware of a cry for help. At first I thought the cry was coming from my own body, with which I was no longer connected—perhaps it was. Soon that one cry merged with a thousand, then ten thousand times ten thousand other cries all calling out in one voice: *Help me! Help me! Help me!* As I focused on that sea of suffering, I became increasingly aware of a sense of self. And I was borne to another realm of existence.

The realm in which I found myself was that of the hungry ghosts. It was a place of horrendous suffering, an overwhelming sea of pain and craving. That realm was like a magnet, drawing into it beings lost in greed and desire. At the same time, these beings were creating this realm out of their insatiable desires. They were enslaved by their desperate attempts to allay the hunger and thirst that preoccupied their whole existence, mistakenly thinking that by satisfying these cravings they would find happiness. They did not know of the deep peace that comes as a result of having given up desires. Ironically and sadly, they were attracted to and supporting the very hell that was the source of their anguish. It was clear to me that those beings did not want to leave their realm—even though they were suffering terribly—any more than those of us who suffer in this realm would want to leave it, that is, want to die.

An old man in a tattered brown tunic came over to me, walking deliberately, leaning on a staff. He recognized me, and I sensed that I knew him too, though I could not remember having met him before. There were many children and adults with swollen bellies and with mouths tight in knots yearning for food and water. My ears were filled with the moans of beings tortured by thirst and hunger and wanting help. These hungry ghosts were trapped in a self-perpetuating wheel of suffering, a wheel that seemed to have no beginning and no end. The old man looked confident and wise. His eyes shone with gentle kindness. I looked at him intently but could not understand why he was there. I longed to do something to alleviate the catastrophic pain I saw around me, but the power of what I was witnessing was too much to bear. Since I was not held by the pull of that realm, I was able to see it clearly as the torment it truly embodied. I reached back into the realm I was most familiar with, the earthly realm, and pleaded with all my heart for help. I became aware of those chanting on my behalf, and suddenly it was as if there were a thousand hands reaching into that dismal place, lifting me up. I felt the support of my Zen teacher, the sangha, and others who were chanting for me, and the love of friends and family who were praying for me.

My whole being then confirmed a phrase I had heard many times: chanting can indeed penetrate seen and unseen realms. I was now drawn to a serene and peaceful realm. To my surprise there were animals as well as humans and what seemed to be buddhas or bodhisattvas in this place of tranquillity and wisdom. The quiet and stillness were palpable. Even the elephants, lions, and birds seemed immobilized, stilled by the power of concentration of the being who was giving a talk. He or she (I never got close enough to tell) was the focal point and central force of this realm. Hundreds of beings were seated in a group listening intently. Back where the animals were sitting or lying still, alert, and waiting, I found a quiet place next to a lion and lay down. A sensation of my "self" was increasing and with it came a feeling of weight and fatigue. I suspect this was due to a growing awareness of and a reassociation with my sick body back in ICU. My affinity with this body was not yet over, and feeling a pull, I grew tired and heavy.

The old man I had seen in the hungry ghost realm appeared in the distance through a hazy veil, but he was held back, from entering this realm of purity and light by his desire not to leave the familiarity of his own realm and the beings he felt strongly connected to. He was smiling, as if the chanting we had tuned in to had soothed him and helped him find a way out of his bondage, but still, he was unable to leave. There was no doubt in my mind that the chanting had indeed helped. It was as if a curtain from one realm to the other had been lifted and the old man was standing somewhere between the two realms. Perhaps in the future he could enter this peaceful realm when he found himself ready and with the confidence to leave.

I vowed never to lose my connection with the old man or others in that realm. I know now with absolute certainty that the chanting and prayers we offer are a very real way of helping all beings suffering in all realms. The karma of those in pain is such that without our help, it would take much longer for them to become free by expiating the root causes of their suffering. In the same way that we are helped by the efforts of highly developed spiritual beings in this and other realms, we too can help other beings in the "lower realms." Really, it is our responsibility to help in whatever way we can. By doing so we are repaying our debt of gratitude for all the help we are receiving and have received since the beginningless beginning.

As I lay next to the lion, resting and becoming more and more exhausted, I felt a strong pull from the ground beneath me, and I was drawn back into my body on that small bed in a room full of pumps and IV bags. I hadn't realized until that moment what an unpleasant thing the body was, especially when one is drugged, full of infection, on a respirator, and so near death. For the first time in days, I opened my eyes. Sunyana-sensei was chanting, standing at my bedside. Tears of gratitude rolled down my face and into my ears. I knew she understood. I wanted to tell her of my experience but was too weak and unable to speak. It felt to me that she had called me back.

When I did eventually come to, as soon as I had the strength to place my hands palm-to-palm, I took a vow to chant every day to help those beings I had met during those days in ICU. Now, whenever I chant wholeheartedly, I can feel the presence of that old man. Perhaps we'll meet again some day.

When the dharma talk was almost finished, I reassured the sangha that I was quite aware of the fact that all mind states, and dreams in particular, were delusive. Even this very life of ours is dreamlike. Nevertheless, suffering and pain can seem very real to one who is experiencing them. This is why when Ramana Maharshi, one of India's great spiritual teachers, was asked whether such realms and beings from other realms were "real," he replied that they were, in fact, "as real as you!" All formations of consciousness seem real to the one experiencing them. The realms we find ourselves in after death—like this realm we now find ourselves in—although illusory, will seem real enough when we are within them. Pleasurable states, states of hunger or thirst, hellish states, sensations of pain, and the horror of it all will be far too concrete to those who find themselves reborn in these realms.

Back home after the dharma talk, the next few days were difficult ones for Margaret and me. I was finding it hard to commit to the transplant. I could not decide to choose a path that I knew would bring so much suffering into my life and the lives of those close to me. Was it worth it?

I called Sensei and discussed the reasons for accepting a path that was guaranteed to lead to pain and suffering, when it might only provide the possibility of a few more years of life. Sunyanasensei reaffirmed my feelings that this illness was an unparalleled opportunity to work through some difficult karma that had ripened and was appearing in my life in this form. For emotional support, I met with Ian, Ross, and Randy and discussed in detail the possible side effects and my chances of survival. Again my family, friends, and Zen teacher reassured me that I would not have to face this ordeal alone. I had no idea of the length they would go to to fulfill their promises. I booked a date for the transplant.

In early December I was readmitted to St. Michael's Hospital for my third round of chemotherapy. I set up an altar in my hospital room and prepared myself for the next onslaught of treatments. Often when I got discouraged I asked Margaret to call her mom's sister. Aunt Marg was a spry eighty-three-year-old, and I found her encouragement and indomitable spirit a wonderful support. She was the first person I saw when I left ICU. She was standing in the hall with fist waving, admonishing me to keep on fighting. Each time I felt a need for inspiration and requested a visit, she would hop on the subway and come to my bedside, always with amusing and uplifting stories.

My mom and her sister, my Aunt Evelyn, came to spend a few days with me. The cycle of visits began, my family each taking their turn, and my friends from the Zen Centre visiting every day. Sunyana-sensei came each time she was in Toronto. How they all managed to make time to visit me regularly and still keep up with their demanding lives I'll never know, but I will always be grateful.

Often Ross, Ian, or Randy would show up early in the morning before work to join me for coffee. There were many times I could not join in the java-fest, but I always appreciated the visits. One morning Ross showed up quite early and, with coffee in hand, told me that it was his twentieth wedding anniversary. He said that he and his wife were going out to dinner with Randy, Ian, and their wives. He knew I wished I were well enough to join them and he told me about the presentation he had planned for that evening. He showed me pictures illustrating how he and his wife, Kathryn, had met and about the early days of their romance. He had done a wonderful job collecting photos and putting together the warm and humorous story he would tell the group that evening. By showing me the pictures and telling me the story, Ross made me feel part of their celebration.

Within days I was confined to my room in isolation, and the counts began to fall. I was hoping that by some stroke of luck I would be home for Christmas, but it seemed unlikely. From past experience I counted the days and realized that I would not be well enough to leave until December 28 at best. But I could still hope.

Margaret was home with the children, since my brother and sister were coming to spend a few days with me. Mike and Shirley-Anne traveled through the worst snowstorm in decades. The highway was closed behind them but they managed to find their way by following a snowplow until it went into a ditch. I was watching the news about the hazardous weather, wondering if they would ever show up, when their smiling faces brightened my room.

We were all confident that I would do much better for this round of chemo because I was much stronger. I did not expect things to decline so quickly. Late that evening I began to experience intense pains in my side. My body broke into a sweat and I was thrown into the fetal position in agony. My brother and sister summoned the doctor for help.

I could not avoid thinking of the woman with swollen hands and feet whom I had visited my last time in the hospital. The bed I was now in was the one she had occupied when her liver began to cause her intolerable pain. She died within a week. This could be it, I told myself. Am I ready?

Mike and Shirley-Anne accompanied me to have my stomach and gallbladder x-rayed. The x-rays were inconclusive and the medical team on call could only hope that the painkilling drugs would minimize my pain until the next day.

Sleep eluded me that night. The pain was unbearable, and I spent the night crouched on my bed with teeth and fists clenched, longing for release. The drugs made me feel stoned but could not reach the intense pain deep in my body. I turned to the doctor after he administered painkillers and, disoriented and confused from the drugs, asked if I could borrow his plane. He didn't own a plane, and I don't know how to fly, but that didn't matter. I wanted to revisit our cabin up north—I was so tired of being in the hospital. I cried and vomited violently. The bright green bile that was ejected was a sign that my gallbladder was malfunctioning.

I slept for a very short time, or passed out from the drugs, and awoke in the middle of the night, feeling a little better. I placed my hands in gassho and began death meditation as I had done many times before. *I may be only a few days away from the flames making their way through the pine box and consuming this body. When shall I prepare myself if not now?*

Even though my mind was wandering from the drugs, beneath the sea of turbulence there was calm and peace. With whatever energy I had left I tried to stay aware of that clarity, knowing that once I was dead all kinds of frightening and seductive mind states could appear. After chanting the last four lines of the *Prajñā Paramita* for some time and focusing on the question, Who am I really? I rested, feeling confident that I was doing the best I could under the circumstances to prepare myself for the great transition.

When I awoke early the next morning, I felt better but knew I was not yet out of the woods. Ultrasound diagnosis revealed that my gallbladder needed to be removed. Although there were no stones, the walls were thick and infected. The surgeons came to call. By this time my blood counts had hit rock bottom and this made me feel very weak. I was still nauseated from the chemotherapy and just beginning to experience its agonizing side effects.

Like many other hospitals, St. Michael's is a training hospital for new physicians. A med student came to inspect me. His prods and pokes brought on sharp pain in my abdomen that shot through my back and up to my shoulder. When the surgeon arrived, also in training, he began to repeat the test to confirm the previous doctor's diagnosis. Within a half hour the head of surgery entered accompanied by the first two doctors and began to demonstrate other ways to confirm the diagnosis and ways to test to be sure that there were no other problems complicating things.

At that point I had had enough. I stopped them and said that I could take no more and asked them to get me down to surgery as soon as possible. The head surgeon told me that the new laparoscopic method for gallbladder removal would be far less painful than the old way and the incisions would be much smaller. When he was leaving my room he noticed the chart on my wall. He looked to the other two doctors and said, "Did you see this? His platelets are below twenty and his white count is almost nil."

"Will that complicate things?" I asked.

"Well, in your case, we will have to be very careful of infections and internal bleeding," he replied.

"You just make damn sure they wash the knives," I said jokingly. They all gave me reassuring smiles. As they left my room I heard the head surgeon say in a low voice to the other two doctors, "I wouldn't touch this guy, not with his blood counts like this."

My brother and sister had to leave and Margaret returned to be with me. That night the tremors of pain came in waves that made the previous night's ordeal seem like only a minor preview. I had thought that things could not possibly get worse. Again I was vomiting bile and experiencing agonizing pain that no amount of drugs seemed to reach. Several times I summoned the nurse to request a doctor. Each time she took one look at my face and literally ran from the room to get help. It was a night I'll never forget.

Margaret looked down at me while I was in spasms, with clenched teeth and grunting from the pain, and said, "You know, I could never do this."

"It's not that difficult when you've got no choice," I replied.

As I lay there I was thinking of all beings who were suffering. I prayed with all my heart that they would find release. Over and over in my mind I repeated, "May all beings find peace." I found the Buddhist verse of repentance arising within me.

> All evil actions committed by me since time immemorial,
> stemming from greed, anger, and ignorance,
> arising from body, speech, and mind,
> I now repent having committed.

Somehow in that focused, attentive moment I was aware that my own past deeds had contributed to the overall suffering of all beings and that working through this karma at this time was a way of helping others. There were other times during the long nights when the pain was so intense that I just lay and waited for release, knowing that eventually "this too shall pass." Ever present, focused, and becoming pain. Often I would lose myself in the pain. As strange as it may sound, there was liberation and freedom in the center of the hurricane. Roshi Kapleau writes in *The Wheel of Life and Death*:

> Some kinds of pain are so all-consuming that one's sense of separation, one's ideas of who one is, one's clinging to all manner of things, disappear into that primordial fire of pain; nothing else exists.[1]

The next morning, completely drained, I insisted upon seeing my hematologist. When he arrived I told him that I had heard the surgeon's remarks and asked what he suggested they do. I knew I could not possibly survive another night like the last one.

"They can't operate, Jim. It is just too risky," he told me. "What we can do is insert a tube to drain the gallbladder. Hopefully this will alleviate the pressure. This method will minimize bleeding and chances of infection. When your counts come up, we can get you into surgery and remove the gallbladder." He then told me that with this method of relieving the pressure it would still take a few days before I would find release from the pain. They arranged for surgery that afternoon.

Although I was somewhat nervous and afraid, I wanted to have the procedure to be free of the pain, which was, by then, constant.

Once I was cleaned and scrubbed, the surgeon told me that they would be inserting the tube through the liver and that the membrane that surrounds the liver is very sensitive to pain. He said that he would not be able to numb the liver as it was a vascular organ, nor could he sedate me during the procedure. Once the tube was inserted, they would increase the painkilling drugs, but they did not want me passing out or vomiting during the operation. He warned me that it was going to be extremely painful. Still, I was not prepared for what was to come.

He placed a long, thick needle on the right side of my abdomen about an inch or so below my ribs and began to hammer it through the liver. Several times I brought my legs and head up from the intense pain. Each time I moved he told me to lie still, my movements were making his work more difficult. But the contractions were uncontrollable.

"I'm sorry, Mr. Bedard," he said several times, "but we can't put you out. Your platelet count is too low." I looked up at the bag of platelets on the IV pole and wondered if my body would retain them this time. I knew how essential they were to help the liver repair itself and to help prevent my body from bleeding excessively.

At one point after being told to lie still yet again, I raised my voice to the surgeon and said, "Why don't you lie here on the table and try not to move while I hammer a needle through your liver." He apologized and I begged him to hurry and get it over with as quickly as possible. I was glad I had asked Margaret to wait in my room. My parents and Cindy-Lee were coming to visit and I wanted someone there to greet them. I knew it would have been very hard on Margaret had she been waiting in the hall, as I was crying out in pain and no longer cared what anyone thought of my pleas to hasten the procedure and get it over with.

When I returned to my room, Margaret, my sister, and my parents were waiting for me. Upon seeing them, I burst into tears and told them that it was the worst experience of my life. "I can't even tell you about it," I said in a weak voice. "It was so awful, you wouldn't believe it." We all cried.

My hematologist came to see me and I told him about the excruciating pain as they inserted the needle through my liver. He told me that my platelets were still at a critical level and that had he known that they were going to go through the liver he would not have allowed the procedure to take place.

"Well, then, I'm glad they didn't tell you," I said, "as there is no way I could have spent another night like the last few." Then, pointing to the bag full of dark red blood that hung from my side, I asked, "Do you think there is a problem with the liver? There is certainly a lot of blood collecting in that bag."

He could see the concern on my face and the faces of my family. He reassured us that the bleeding had let up some and that as long as I did not pick up an infection I would be fine. Within a day or two the liquid in the bag became clearer, indicating that my liver was healing. But my white blood cell count was still nil and an infection would be dangerous.

Late that night I spiked a fever. The doctors began administering antibiotics, and I weakened quickly, experiencing chills and shivering, then becoming hot and sweaty. My family was with me the next morning when the infectious-disease specialist told us, again, that he thought the central venous catheter line was infected and would have to be removed. When he left my room I sank into the bed, trying to disappear. I could not possibly take any more.

I looked at my wife, my sister, and my parents. I felt as if I were somehow letting them down. For me, the news was devastating. I had no fight left in me nor did I want any. I was giving up. The pain of the last few days had sapped my already weakened body-mind, and I could no longer summon up the strength to face the day and the upcoming challenges. Months of illness and the intense pain of the past several days were taking their toll.

"I can't believe it," I cried. "After all I've been through, there is no way I'm going to make it. How can I possibly get through another Hickman line operation, then have my gallbladder out, while preparing myself for another round of chemo and radiation that they warned me would be far worse than anything I've experienced already? I have all this to look forward to and I still have to prepare myself for a bone marrow transplant. There's no way I can do it. I can't even bring myself to think about it. I think I'm losing the battle here."

I hung my head and sobbed. I had hit rock bottom.

Within the hour, the doctor on call told me I had a touch of pneumonia. When one is confined to bed for days and unable to sit up, infections often settle in the lungs. I was heading for the respirator again and the ICU ward, but for a short time I didn't care.

I looked over at my mom and sister; they were trying to encourage Margaret, telling her not to worry, that I would be able to get over this next hurdle. *They all have so much faith in me, I thought. If only I could find such faith at times like this.*

I felt like a fighter who was down for the count and the spectators were shouting encouragements and pleas to get up, to stay in there, to keep fighting. People kept telling me not to give up, but I wondered how anyone else could possibly know how difficult it was to keep going. I felt isolated, as if I had no allies. Without a doubt, my family, friends, and teacher would do whatever they could to help, and yet I knew that I would have to live through this alone.

As I lay there, I asked myself the ultimate question: *Am I going to decide to fight, can I decide to fight, to choose life, or is this it?* It was clear to me that if things did not change for the better very soon, I would again be in critical condition and perhaps facing death. I wondered whether or not Sensei really knew what she was asking of me when she encouraged me to choose life at every turn. Then I thought of my children, not knowing if I was blessed or cursed to have thoughts of my love for them surface at a time like this. Thinking of them growing up without a father was not an option. Although I had known all along what I had to do and, indeed, what I was going to do, contemplating my situation gave me the resolve and determination to take the next step.

"Well," I said to my concerned guests, "let's get on with it.

Margaret, Mom, Cindy-Lee, help me get these covers off. We have work to do."

Cindy-Lee immediately began to cry, and my father disappeared behind his newspaper. My mother and Margaret began helping me remove the covers. I knew that getting up and off my back would help my failing lungs recover. I struggled to my feet and began walking back and forth in the room supported by my mother and Margaret.

"We've been here a few times before, eh, honey?" my mother said in an encouraging tone.

"Yes, Mom, and it probably won't be the last," came my reply.

With tear-stained cheeks, IV pole in hand, and with a bag of bile pinned to my side, I stepped onto the road to recovery. I was soon coughing a lot, which flexed the abdominal muscles and moved the line through the liver. It was quite painful, but it helped. Just being on my feet offered reassurance to those attending me and gave me the inspiration I needed to believe I could do it. With the support of loved ones, I kept on walking.

At times I wondered why I had decided to carry on. The tears that came to the eyes of those watching me, and my thoughts of my family, my teacher, and my friends, reminded me that this was just a low moment and that I would be grateful some day that I had decided to make the effort. One foot in front of the other, no past, no future. I sought freedom in the present.

When I was alone again, I felt the crushing weight of the challenges that lay ahead. When they were crowded together, they seemed insurmountable for me. Even taking things one day at a time seemed to be more than I could handle. So I broke the day into pieces—mornings only, afternoons only, evenings only. I told myself early in the day, *You have to make it until noon, that's all. You can do it. Don't think of anything else but from now till lunch.* Then in the afternoon I would take the piece until dinner, and so on.

I did my best not to think of the operations that lay ahead, the possibility of full-blown pneumonia, the respirator, the infected line, or the bone marrow transplant. Instead I focused only on the next immediate step. I reminded myself again and again to remain in the present. Freedom from confusion and despair came from focusing on and living in the moment. Practicing being completely present was familiar to me. *The present, this very moment, however dismal, this is where I must take refuge,* I told myself. Again I was on a tightrope, one step at a time. With whatever focus I had left, I attempted to experience the present only. Days no longer days, hours no longer hours, no thoughts of minutes or of time.

The drugs assailed my concentration and brought states of confusion. I began to wrestle with the question of whether to take painkillers, which offered a bit of respite but disturbed the mind, or put up with the agony and maintain some clarity of mind. Often the answer that came was simple: Wait it out, see it through; this too shall pass.

No matter how hard I tried to remain focused, life for the next week was an unremitting struggle with despair. The downward spiral came every time I let my guard down for even a moment. Then, just as if I were pushing a large stone up a hill, I would struggle to regain some measure of confidence, a positive attitude, and enough resolve to carry on.

Late one night after hours of being unable to sleep, my spirits sank. Too weak to pull myself together, I experienced the fall and watched to see where it would lead. I felt as if there were a deep crack somewhere inside and life was oozing out of me. *I need help,* I thought. *If I allow this to continue, surely I'll never find my way back.*

It was 2:00 A.M. and I felt uncomfortable asking for help at such an ungodly hour. Finally I called Margaret, who was staying in a residence nearby.

"What is it?" she asked.

"I think I need a hot bowl of soup," I replied. Then I began to cry.

"I'll be right there," she reassured me.

Margaret brought hot soup, but I couldn't eat. We talked for a while, then I asked her to call Eric, who lived in Victoria, as it was three hours earlier there. It was a good move. Eric had experience with coming off drugs from his hippie days in the sixties. I don't think he ever would have thought this would come in handy helping someone. He reminded me that the turbulent mind states were drug induced and that the more attention I paid to them the more real they would seem. His advice made a lot of sense.

"You sound like Sensei," I said. "I know what you're saying, Eric. I've been there a thousand times while practicing, but I can't concentrate when I'm drugged and feeling so depressed."

Just talking to him made a big difference. He told me about his latest magic tricks and his new contracts, reeled off a few jokes, and had me laughing. Next I talked to both John and Michael and was soon exhausted and ready for sleep. Margaret returned to the residence so we could both get some rest. Still, I could not sleep.

The pump administering my antibiotics kept beeping every few minutes, preventing me from falling asleep. The nurses brought in a different pump, but the replacement turned out to be noisier than the previous one. The constant buzzing and clicking made rest impossible. On that night the sound seemed more invasive than ever. Some pumps were noisier than others, and by a stroke of misfortune I was hooked up to one of the worst. I summoned the nurse several times, asking her to adjust it so I could rest. I really needed to rest. She tried to get the pump running properly, but it was impossible.

"I'm going to unplug it and get some peace and quiet," I said.

"You can't, Jim, you really need these medications. I'm sorry, but this is the only pump available to us for now. We can get you one that works better in the morning when maintenance arrives."

"You're right about my needing the meds," I said, "but I need rest more. Please just disconnect the pump or I'm going to clamp the lines when you leave and shut the damn thing off. I'm at the end of my rope. I need rest more than anything."

I had spent a large part of the last four months on that floor and the nurses and I had gotten to know each other fairly well. They considered me pretty easygoing even at the worst of times. This was different. It was 4:00 A.M. and I had slept off and on for only a few hours in days. The nurse knew I wasn't kidding and that I desperately needed rest. She unplugged the pump, and eventually I drifted off to sleep.

The next morning, about forty minutes after shift change, I awoke to find the same nurse reconnecting a new pump. "Are you working a double shift?" I asked, surprised to see her still there.

"No, I stayed late so you could get some rest. See how much we care about you here? I've informed the day shift that you are behind schedule with your medications, and they'll help you get caught up so none of us loses our job. Hope this pump works better for you. Now I'm getting out of here while I can. It's my turn to get some rest."

I thanked her over and over, but I still wonder if she ever knew how much I appreciated the break she awarded me on that night.

Realizing that my stubborn self-reliance would make things more difficult for me in the long run, I spoke to Ian, Ross, and Randy. I told them of my episode the previous night and about wanting to call them but resisting because it was so late. They were adamant that they wanted to do more and that my calling them, especially at night, was a way of giving them that opportunity.

"Jim, you have to appreciate how difficult this is for us. We often wish we could do more and at times we feel so helpless. Please give us the chance, it will make it easier for us. We want to help. We need to help."

It was what I needed to hear. I knew in my heart that it was I who was making things worse for myself. *Damn pride*, I thought, *another subtle form of attachment to self.* I knew I needed to practice humility. There was no way I was going to be able to face the upcoming challenges without the help of my family, my Zen teacher, and my dear friends.

From that point on I felt very comfortable being open in asking for support and being honest when I felt the need to be alone. It took hitting bottom to shatter some deeply held self-images, but the freedom that followed allowed me to weather some very trying times with less fear and less self-consciousness. For those with a strong sense of self, it's very difficult to ask for help. In fact, it takes selflessness and humility to do so. Sensei often told me that one is actually doing others a favor by asking them for help. Most people naturally want to help others and just need to be shown how.

The pain and weakness continued. I ate little for the next several days, but soon my counts began to climb. The doctors told me that my pneumonia had cleared up and that as soon as my platelet count was above thirty, I would be allowed to return home. The gallbladder surgery would be booked once my blood counts were stable. Patients often recover from chemo more quickly in subsequent treatments. There was still a possibility of my being home for the holidays.

The next week the chart on the wall offered some encouraging signs. However, the platelet count was slow to rise. My body was again having a hard time keeping the counts above twenty. John was visiting, and as my white count was up slightly, I was released from isolation and given permission to roam the halls. It was December 19.

When I left my room for the first time in weeks, I was mesmerized by the bright and colorful Christmas decorations. John and I were feeling very emotional—when it came time for him to leave, I could see that he was having difficulty. When he got to the door he turned and said, "Damn it, Jim, you know I've been here a lot off and on since August. But then for me it's back to life as usual. I can't believe you're still here, that you've been here all along. It seems like such a long time ago that we were all here and you were just being admitted. Are you sure you're okay? I really don't

want to leave you here. God, I wish I could take you with me."
He turned away, not wanting me to see his tears.

I said in a broken voice, "Don't worry about me, pal, I'll be
okay. Really, I'm just a little emotional with all this Christmas stuff
happening. This last week or two has taken a lot out of me. It
almost broke me, John. I don't know how I'm going to face the
next phase."

We stood for a moment in silence and hugged for a long time.
Neither of us could speak. He walked to the door several times
before actually leaving. Looking out my hospital window on the
seventh floor, I watched him make his way through the parking
lot to his car. I could see people going shopping and offering each
other season's greetings. I went to the bed, turned my face into
the pillow, and cried. I felt so alone.

I was rescued by angels singing in the hall. I wondered whether
I was hallucinating. I had never heard a choir sound so beautiful.
The ching, ching, of the tambourine introduced Christmas carols. A
nurse came into my room and encouraged me to come and see the
children singing. They were adorable and their voices breathtak-
ing. But for some reason, every time I made it to the door and saw
their beaming faces, red vests, and joyful demeanor, I broke into
tears and returned to my bed. Nevertheless, the spell of loneliness
was broken.

Several times a day when blood was taken, I asked for my
counts. December 20, and still my platelet count was hovering
around the low twenties. Although my side felt much better, I was
discouraged to hear that my platelets would have to come up to
thirty before the doctors would even consider letting me leave for
home.

That night Margaret asked me to join her in the waiting room.
When I entered the decorated room, our children called out, "Surprise! Merry Christmas!" They told me that they were staying for
the holidays. One of Toronto's best hotels, the Royal York, gave us

two rooms free of charge. They generously made this offer to families of patients who could not go home for Christmas.

A couple of close friends from Windsor visited that day. As they were leaving, they asked me how I was going to pay for my family's meals. I told them, "I have no idea," and walked with them to the elevator. When I returned to my room, I was astonished to find a card propped on my pillow. I opened it to find several hundred dollars. That same day, another close friend from Windsor called and said that he wanted to cover my family's holiday expenses. I couldn't imagine how I would ever be able to thank these friends enough.

My counts climbed daily. On December 24, at 1:00 P.M., with a platelet count of twenty-nine, I was given permission to leave the hospital. The lines coming from my heart were capped. I was given instructions on how to care for the exit site of the line coming from the gallbladder and showed how to empty the bag of bile hanging from my side. We headed home to Bethany.

While I was in the hospital, the local church had welcomed our kids into their programs and had given them support even though we were not members. That night our children participated in a Christmas play, and a tired, proud, skinny, bald man wearing a bandana sat in the congregation watching. The carols and stories during the service were as welcome as the many hugs I received from the community afterward. Before leaving, we enjoyed hot apple cider and Christmas cake.

As we drove away from the church I was thinking, *Perhaps this is the way it's going to be: pain, illness, hurdles and challenges that I won't expect, and then more of the same, with little rest in between. So be it, I thought. What a wonderful night it is anyway.*

8

THE GIFT

I know well enough these
Cherry blossoms will
Return to dust, but I
Find it hard to leave
The trees in full bloom.

—JAPANESE WAKA POEM

THE NEW YEAR WAS DAWNING. Without any expectations of how things should be or how they might turn out, I felt a great peace arise within. It was truly joyful to be home with my parents, Margaret, and my children for the holidays.

I knew that many more challenges awaited me and that I had come close to breaking this time. The intense pain after so many months of hospitalization and illness had worn me down. I vowed to use all my resources, everything in my power, to stay positive mentally and emotionally. Looking back over the entire ordeal, it seemed that the moments of discouragement were the most difficult of all. I needed to prepare for the time ahead. Gallbladder surgery, intensive chemotherapy and radiation, the bone marrow transplant—any of these could cause death. It was going to take a strong spirit to be able to face these hurdles with composure and confidence.

My life took on a new sense of urgency. Whenever I had the energy to do so I sat in zazen to contemplate the "great matter of birth and death." My chanting gained strength and my concentration deepened daily.

I spent the first few days of the New Year resting and enjoying visits from family and friends. Although I had little strength, I slept better and could again taste food. A week or two after the holidays Shirley-Anne called to say that she and her partner, Marc, had just completed their home zendo. She wanted to know if I could join them for a dedication ceremony.

Eric was in town. He and I met Randy, Ross, and Ian in Toronto and headed to North Bay. My mother and Shirley-Anne spent the day preparing delicious, spicy vegetarian Indian dishes. My other siblings and their spouses all joined us for dinner. After we had eaten and were having tea, I said, "I would have to be in denial not to realize that there's a chance that I may not make it through these next treatments and the transplant. I wanted to be sure to have the opportunity to express my love and my deepest gratitude for your support. Thank you so much. You should know that I have a new resolve in my heart and I plan to do my best to stay as positive as I possibly can. I'm sure I'll survive the ordeal, I hope I'll survive the ordeal. Surely you know I'm feeling very apprehensive, but knowing that you're going to be there for me is making this a lot easier." We had a fine evening. My family and friends offered encouraging words and reaffirmed their support. It was a warm time, and the room was often filled with laughter and tears.

The next morning my friends joined Eric and me at the dedication of the new zendo. My niece Lee-Anne carried an incense bowl into the room to the sound of gongs. Randy intoned the chants, and a short procession entered. We lit incense, offered flowers and fruit, and installed a Buddha figure on the new altar. Then we sat in zazen and dedicated our spiritual practice to the welfare of all sentient beings.

Resting in the back of the van as we returned to Bethany, I felt like the luckiest man in the world. I had been born into a fine family; I had a lovely wife and four beautiful children; I had wonderful friends; I had found the Buddha's teaching and was practicing with a fine teacher and sangha. With a couple of tubes coming out of my chest and a bag of bile hanging from my side, I was full of gratitude. I felt whole. My life felt so complete that even death could not diminish it.

Surgery was upcoming in a couple of weeks and the transplant was set for February 29. I was looking forward to a break to prepare myself for the approaching ordeal. The terrible pain I had undergone had really taken its toll, and I was anticipating spending time resting and recuperating at home.

During the next week I was again assaulted with several liver and gallbladder attacks. Feeling that I just couldn't take it anymore, I called the hospital and insisted that they operate sooner. They moved my surgery up one week, but that was still ten days away.

My friends from the Zen Centre and Sensei were preparing for the January Rohatsu sesshin. This is a seven-day retreat to commemorate the Buddha's enlightenment and is one of the most important times of the year for a Buddhist. The following week I went to the opening ceremony of the sesshin and planned to attend the first two days before having my gallbladder surgery. The sesshin began with a special ceremony of gratitude for the Buddha's teachings. There were readings, chanting, and of course zazen.

During sesshin one is normally required to stay at the center, but because of my health I spent the evening with Randy and his wife, Marielle, who lived nearby. We had planned to return the next morning to hear Sensei's talk, but just before we were about to leave, I fell to the floor in the worst gallbladder attack I had ever experienced. I called to Randy and he rushed into my room. He saw that I had broken out in a sweat and was doubled over on the floor. Scarcely able to speak, I asked him to call the hospital to see if they would take me that day. To my dismay, they told him to give me some painkillers until surgery the next day.

I was only half a mile from the center while a talk was being given by my teacher, yet I was unable to be there. I wanted so much to be at sesshin, absorbing its strengthening power in preparation for surgery and the upcoming transplant. But it was not to be. The pain kept me confined to Randy and Marielle's home. Any moment could be my last and I wanted to keep practice with me each step of the way.

Early the next day Randy drove me to St. Michael's Hospital and I was admitted and prepped for gallbladder surgery. When I awoke afterward, I found Margaret, Bradley, and Raymond sitting by my side. I was very sick and spent most of the night vomiting, experiencing terrible abdominal pain and nausea.

The next day I was in less pain, although still feeling very sick. I was surprised to hear that I was being sent home that day. I told the nurse that I was still very nauseated and did not feel strong enough to be leaving the hospital. "Perhaps I should stay for at least another day or two," I suggested. My request was turned down. With bowl in hand, still vomiting, I walked the hall toward the elevator feeling unimpressed with this perfunctory treatment. Until that day I had nothing but good words to say about the hospitals and the care I had received.

Late that night at home in Bethany I awoke with terrible pain in my side, my body again convulsed in spasms. Margaret was sleeping in another room because she was worried about accidentally bumping into the incisions in my abdomen. I tried to call out through clenched teeth but the pain and spasms made it impossible. I hit the wall with my arm several times and grunted as loud as I could. Margaret soon heard my primitive calls for help.

"What should I do? What should I do? What's the matter?" Margaret frantically asked.

"C- c- ca- call . . ." I couldn't speak; the pain was too severe.

My body was frozen in the fetal position in a vain attempt to protect itself from the onslaught. I relaxed into the pain for a brief moment and whispered to Margaret, "Call an ambulance."

"Are you sure? Perhaps I should call St. Mike's first to see what they think."

I didn't speak but continued to fight off the pain, looking up at Margaret. Margaret looked into my eyes and understood at once. "I'll call an ambulance," she said.

The ride to the hospital in Peterborough was excruciating. Each bump in the road tore into my side and made me realize I should have insisted upon staying at the hospital.

At emergency I was immediately given drugs to help with the pain. I guided the nurses through the doses and types of painkillers that experience had taught me would work best and not cause me to vomit. Margaret left to register me, and a nurse who was unfamiliar with Hickman lines came to take a blood sample. She carried a book on central venous catheters, opened it, placed it on my thighs, and looking at the diagrams, began to remove one of the caps to my line. The drugs had started to bring some relief. My mind was growing hazy, but I was alert enough to know that she was doing something wrong.

"Don't! You can't do that," I said. "Air will get into the line."

"Oh, I'm sorry," she said and turned a few pages to another section of the book.

The drugs were drawing me into a fog of incoherence, but I was aware enough to be alarmed. I demanded that she wait until Margaret was present. Several times I insisted that she stop, until eventually she left, frustrated and annoyed. She told Margaret that I would not let her proceed until she was there. I was concerned that if I passed out the nurse might make another error. After all I had been through I did not want to die because of an avoidable mistake by someone inexperienced with Hickman lines.

It was fortunate that I insisted Margaret be there. When the nurse drew blood from my line, Margaret noticed that she was using the wrong gauge needle, one that was far too large for the rubber cap. After obtaining the sample, the nurse left the blood in the line without flushing it. Margaret and I both knew that the blood would soon clot and plug the line. If this happened, the line would need to be replaced surgically, or even worse, it might force a clot into my heart or lungs, where it could cause very serious problems. We asked the nurse to please quickly get us some solution to flush the lines. We gave her the name of the drug we needed and the needle size, and off she went. We sat waiting nervously, looking at lines full of blood. Suddenly Margaret remembered that she still had syringes and solution in her purse from when we traveled up north to see my folks.

"Let's do it," I said, "but we have to hurry. I can hardly see I'm so stoned."

When the nurse returned (again with the wrong size needles) she sat and watched me as I tried to focus my eyes and mind long enough to do the job. I managed to flush the lines and replace the damaged cap. Then I clamped the lines and passed out.

Within an hour, I was again in terrible pain and experiencing spasms. They gave me more drugs while waiting for the surgeon to arrive. Soon the surgeon, an elderly, distinguished-looking man, came over to my bed and introduced himself.

"Something is wrong, doc. I'm in terrible pain. They must have taken out the wrong part. I'm sure I'm having a gallbladder attack. Trust me, I know what it feels like."

He got on the phone and called the hospital where the surgery was done and then returned to reassure me that they had indeed taken out the right part.

"But, Jim," he said, "they also did a liver biopsy, and with your platelets being so low, I suspect there may be some internal bleeding. The pressure in the liver area from the bleeding is causing pain similar to a gallbladder attack. There is also a possibility of a stone being lodged in one of the bile ducts that they didn't see when doing the surgery. We'll do an ultrasound to be sure."

The ultrasound was inconclusive but the surgeon felt that internal bleeding was causing the problem. I was put into a private room and hooked up to a pump. The familiar-looking pump, which administered saline solution to keep my lines open and to keep me hydrated, was a very noisy one. Again I could get no rest. I asked for the pump to be shut off. The nurses on night shift agreed, since the saline solution could drip by gravity.

The pain stayed with me for the rest of that day and into the night, with little release. At some point during the night, when I felt I could take no more, I called the nurse. "Would you please page my surgeon?" I asked. "This pain is unbearable. There is no way I can possibly go through another night like last night."

"I'm sorry, Mr. Bedard. We can't do that. But he did leave us a strong sedative to give you if the pain became intolerable." She gave me something so potent that it completely knocked me out.

The next morning I awoke to someone gently tapping my hand and calling my name. I thought it was my mother or Sunyana-sensei. This was confusing because I knew that neither of them was in Peterborough that day. I opened my eyes, but to my surprise no one else was in the room. I turned my head to look for the person who had awakened me and saw that my IV bag was empty. My IV line was full of air.

"What! Oh, no!" I shouted and immediately clamped my lines and called for help.

When the Hickman line was first installed I had been told what to do if air got into the lines and into the heart. If you lay on one side the air would slowly dissipate; lying on the other side could lead to cardiac arrest. It was essential to know which side to lie on—and I had forgotten.

Damn! I thought. Hurry up, think clearly! Is it the left side or the right side?

I did not have enough faith in the nurses to ask them which side I should lie on. The Peterborough hospital had no oncology ward, so the nurses were unfamiliar with central venous catheters. Earlier that day several of them had asked permission to be present when

I flushed my lines and tended to the exit site, receiving their first lesson in Hickman line care.

The nurses rushed to replace my IV bags and the lines leading to my central venous catheter and brought syringes to help me flush them. We discovered that the saline solution had been about three inches away from my entry site when I was awakened. No air had gotten into the heart, but had I slept another few minutes . . .

The nurse responsible for my ward apologized profusely for forgetting to replace the bag that night. I told her that I was very disappointed, and had I died because of someone's forgetfulness after all I had been through, there would have been an extremely unpleasant ghost inhabiting the halls of that floor for some time.

When the nurses left my room, I calmed down and began to reflect on the gentle tapping of my hand and calling of my name that probably saved my life. *My mother and her angels,* I thought. I didn't have much faith in angels. My mother, on the other hand, had no doubts about them.

I recalled an incident in my childhood that had affected me profoundly. I was about twelve years old and home sick from school during a snowstorm. My father, who was a plasterer, called to say he had forgotten his lunch. Mom wrapped me up warmly and we ventured out into the storm to deliver it to him.

Somehow we got lost and ended up on an old snow-covered, abandoned road. As my mom tried to turn the car around she backed into a ditch. The station wagon sat at a forty-five degree angle with its nose pointing skyward. All attempts to push or rock the car out were unsuccessful. It was stuck fast. I wandered off to look for a pole to try to pry it out. Meanwhile, my mother sat in the car and warmed herself. As I headed back, empty-handed, I heard my mom call to her patron saint in a loud, determined voice, "Saint Jude, get me out of this mess!" Smiling, I thought, *Mom's angry with the gods and they weren't even the ones driving.*

The next instant, as my mom sat with hands clenched on the steering wheel, our car shot out of the ditch and swerved onto the road. My mouth dropped open. It was the most astonishing thing I had ever seen. My mom was convinced that she had been helped by her patron saint, and I was left to wonder about that mysterious afternoon for years. I suspect it is one of the reasons I began looking into spiritual practice as a young adult. No amount of reasoning could satisfy my puzzled mind. What I had seen that day could not be explained rationally.

As I lay in my hospital bed that morning remembering that snowy afternoon years before, I thought to myself, *Wait until Mom and Cindy-Lee hear about this one!* Both of them had often told me that they were praying for their angels to watch over me. Many evenings I also felt my nieces and nephews sending me healing energy. Cindy-Lee later told me that every night after dinner the children would recite the rosary for me.

When I visited my parents a few weeks later I told Cindy-Lee and my mother about my extraordinary experience. They were both sure that one of their angels had awakened me just in time. Cindy-Lee gathered her six children and asked me to tell the story again. The children, who ranged in age from two to twelve, then told me that they, too, had prayed for me that day and had sent their guardian angels off to watch over me. They did this even though they believed this would leave them unprotected. It was such a selfless gesture.

Six-year-old Mary-Kate looked up at me and asked, "Uncle Jimmy, do you have any angels in Buddhism?"

"Well, honey," I said, "we do have bodhisattvas, who are very spiritually advanced and who dedicate their lives to helping others, but not angels with big wings as you know them."

"That's okay, Uncle Jimmy," came her pure-hearted reply. "You can borrow some of ours until you get some of your own."

With a big smile on my face and a heart full of love, I said, "When I return to the hospital the next time, I'm sure I'll need all the help I can get. So please do keep praying for me."

I then hugged all the children and thanked them warmly. Seeing their smiling faces and feeling their selfless love, how could I not believe in angels? Six of them stood wide-eyed looking up at me.

I was at home recuperating from the gallbladder surgery when I got a call to come into Princess Margaret Hospital for a checkup. The nurse told me that I was soon to be admitted to the Princess Margaret Lodge near the hospital to be monitored during my chemotherapy treatments.

"You must be mistaken," I said. "I don't go in until February 29."

"Let me explain to you how it works, Mr. Bedard," she said. "February 29 is 'Day Zero.' That is the actual day of your transplant. We have to count back from there to figure out when to do the pulmonary test, the blood work, and the lumbar puncture and begin the first round of chemotherapy treatments at the lodge."

It was early February and it didn't seem as if I would get the break I was looking forward to. I knew there was little I could do about it and that to get discouraged was only going to make things worse.

Before being admitted to the lodge for preliminary tests I traveled to see my parents and siblings. Just as I was sitting down to tea with John, Shirley-Anne, and my mother, we got a call saying that John was the chosen bone marrow donor. He broke into tears and exclaimed, "It's a miracle! It's a damn miracle!"

We all hugged and cried. I looked at John and felt so grateful to have such a brother. For that matter, any one of my brothers or sisters would have gladly donated their marrow to rescue me. I then told them some stories I had heard of siblings charging their recipients for their marrow.

John replied, "Well, you didn't think I was going to do it for free, did you?" As he wiped the tears from his eyes, he added, "The reason I'm so happy, Jim, is that I know you and Margaret have a great camper and I always wanted a camper of my own."

We had a good laugh, a few warm hugs, and some hot tea served with Mom's Christmas cake and muffins.

After returning to Bethany, I made time to walk every day, do zazen regularly, and chant whenever possible. I tried to keep my mind focused so that I would be able to avoid getting overly discouraged or depressed the next time around. I had met several patients who had gone for their transplants. Some of them had done their chemotherapy at home and had felt quite normal and well prepared mentally and physically going into the transplant. Nevertheless, they told me it had taken everything they had just to make it through. I knew that I was starting out at a disadvantage because of my ordeal over the past six months. I still felt very weak and emotionally drained.

Before I had left St. Michael's Hospital, some of the nurses had wanted to introduce Margaret, my mother, and me to a patient who had just gone through an autologous bone marrow transplant, where the recipient was his own donor. The nurses explained that his procedure was not as challenging as the one I was about to undergo, but they still felt it would be inspiring for me to meet someone who was doing so well after the procedure.

The patient was sitting on his bed, his face and body swollen and his skin a sunburned red. He was very weak but was trying to get out of bed and stand. It was a frightening picture of what was to come. I could not go into the room. Margaret entered and was introduced while my mother waited with me in the hall outside his room. Shortly afterward we heard a round of applause coming from the patient's room. His family was overjoyed that he had taken a few steps. With my head hung slightly I quietly said to Margaret as she joined my mother and me, "Apparently that's the gentler of the two types of transplants, and he's doing so well that they expect me to be encouraged by seeing him. Man, now I really am scared."

The past six months had seemed like years. I felt like a worn-out old veteran. Yet I had a few weeks before the transplant, and I knew it could make a difference. Doing zazen, chanting, taking morning walks and afternoon naps—all slowly began to help me feel confident that I could be ready in time.

A week before I was to be admitted for preliminary chemotherapy at the lodge, I visited the hospital clinic for tests. When the blood results came back, the doctors told me that they were going to have to do a bone marrow aspiration immediately. They suspected that I had relapsed, because my counts had fallen so low. It was one of the longest afternoons of my life. Margaret and I knew they would not have worried us unless they suspected that something was seriously wrong. My mind began racing. *Start all over again? No way! Well, there's no way I'm giving up either, not after all this. Try not to think about it until they have the results.* So, sitting in a chair in a crowded hospital waiting room, I did some very intense zazen.

"Good news, Mr. Bedard," the doctor said. "It looks as though your blood counts may have been low because of an infection. The transplant is still a go."

On the way to the elevators I said to Margaret, "You know, for a while there I was hoping they were going to tell us we couldn't go ahead with the transplant. I'm not sure what it is I wanted to hear, but I'm still having a hard time accepting the fact that I have to go in so soon. I'm afraid of it, Margaret, and I'm not used to being afraid. But no matter what happens, we're committed now. It will be good to get it behind us." Margaret took my hand as we stepped into the elevator.

In mid-February I was admitted to the Princess Margaret Lodge. From there I went to a clinic to be hooked up to a portable chemo pump. It resembled a Walkman, with the tube running directly into my Hickman line. I hadn't known that I would also be having a lumbar puncture. During the procedure, chemotherapy was injected directly into my spine to attack leukemia cells in the central nervous system. Usually there are few or no side effects with spinal chemo, but this was not true in my case. I had to stay horizontal for the next ten days and could eat almost nothing. I was in a daze, assailed by excruciating headaches and constant vomiting.

On February 26 I began intensive chemotherapy at Princess Margaret Hospital. Michael took me to the hospital and stayed to get me settled in my new room. He was unpacking my clothes when I looked at him, completely disoriented. "Where the hell am I, Mike? Is this PMH? When did you get here? What day is it?"

A worried look crept over his face. "Yes, you're at Princess Margaret Hospital, Jim. I picked you up at the lodge and drove you here this morning. Don't you remember?"

"Not really. Oh, yeah. You have a red truck, right?" Mike had a brand-new, fire-engine red pickup truck. All I could remember about the past ten days was that bright red color.

"Mike, I don't feel ready. Not for radiation, more chemo, and a bone marrow transplant. I never had a chance to prepare myself for all this. Look at me. Imagine going into a bone marrow transplant feeling like this. I can't even sit up in bed or keep a bowl of pudding down. Mike, I need you to do me a favor. Would you set up an altar for me? There's a jade Kannon that I brought from home in my bag and some pictures that were gifts from my teacher and some friends."

Mike placed them on the window ledge so that each time I looked out the window and every time I returned to my bed I would face the altar. It would be a constant reminder for me to stay as focused and as positive as possible. He also placed a calender on the wall and marked an X on that day's date, February 26. He then said, "Jim, it won't be too long before you're marking off these days," pointing to the fourth week in March.

The marking of the calendar soon became a joke for my family and me. They insisted that we wait until at least six in the evening before marking off the days. I, on the other hand, wanted to mark them at nine or ten in the morning. Had I been stronger I would have gotten out of bed and marked the calendar myself, I was so anxious to see the days pass. As I looked at that calendar I longed for the day that I would be out of the hospital, with this whole ordeal behind me, feeling much better. Some days I would have Margaret or my mother begin the mark on the calendar in the morning, and they would complete it at 6:00 P.M. A family compromise.

The day I entered PMH, our children arrived in the evening. It was completely unexpected, and I broke into tears. It was wonderful to see them when I was feeling so apprehensive. I no longer doubted my decision to go ahead with the transplant, but I still felt a need for support and encouragement. Seeing their smiling faces always confirmed that I had made the right choice. I was too tired to visit and talk much, but we hugged and I explained some of the new procedures to them.

The room I was confined to was about twelve feet square. It would be my home for the next five weeks. Fortunately, the view was incredible: the windows looked out over Lake Ontario and the west end of Toronto. The wall at the head of my bed was a series of perforated metal panels behind which were numerous air filters. A constant flow of air coming from these panels circulated away from me and around a glass wall to an intake vent. This prevented any germs on visitors or hospital staff from reaching me. Whenever people entered the room they would stand for fifteen seconds in the entranceway with the fans turned on high to "air wash" themselves. It was all very high tech. The bone marrow transplant unit at PMH had opened only three months before, and I felt extremely fortunate to be in a brand-new, state-of-the-art facility. At some hospitals, isolation after a transplant meant that no one except hospital personnel and immediate family could enter the room. Even then, visitors would have to wear protective masks and gowns. At PMH, however, if family and friends were not ill, they could visit without the inconvenience of protective gear.

On February 28 John arrived to begin preparations for the next day's surgery. Later that day, the night before the transplant, he visited my room. I was waiting for him. Margaret had enlarged a wonderful picture of the two of us standing arm in arm outside a bird sanctuary. I had inscribed the back with "John, you and I have always been good friends, and I always knew you loved me dearly, but now I can feel your love in my bones." I had planned to give it to him after his surgery, but I realized he would be drugged, and I had no idea how I might be doing. After I gave him the picture, John and I visited with our parents and Margaret. We were all filled with anxiety but wanted to get it over with.

Day Zero—when I awoke on February 29, John was already in surgery. After I had a light meal, a bag of marrow was brought into my room. The marrow was thicker than the blood I was used to and there were particles floating in the fluid. "How long can that stay unrefrigerated?" I asked. I had not yet had the radiation treatments, which would take at least an hour.

"Don't worry Jim, this stuff is good for about twelve hours," the nurse replied.

Margaret and my mother arrived shortly afterward. My mother stood at the door, white as a ghost, with her hands clenched at her sides. Margaret looked just as worried. "I was doing fine until you two showed up," I said. My heart began to beat faster and a very familiar sinking feeling began to draw me into the sheets. I wondered whether they knew more about what was coming than I did. In a moment attendants arrived to take me to the radiation room. Throughout my months-long ordeal there were only a few times that I felt it would be easier to face the challenges of the day by myself rather than with company. This was one of them.

Total body radiation is painless, but unnerving nonetheless. In a room half the size of a gymnasium, I was placed on a mat on the floor and covered with foam pads. The attendants told me to keep my eyes open throughout the treatment and quickly left. A machine that dwarfed me descended quietly, animated by robotic movements. "Are you okay, Mr. Bedard?" came a voice over the intercom. "If you have a problem, we can hear you." The nurse reassured me that I was not alone, but her words meant little. The sound of that heavy, lead-coated steel door as it closed convinced me that I was indeed alone.

When I returned to my room, the bag of marrow was immediately hooked up to my Hickman line. A nurse sat constantly by my side, periodically checking my temperature, breathing, heart rate, and blood pressure. As I had been told to expect, the transfusion itself was anticlimactic. The marrow was administered in the same way I had received blood products in the past, directly into the central venous catheter. When I asked about how the new marrow would find its way into the bone and engraft, the attending doctor said, "Jim, I don't understand it either. Medicine, too, has to rely on the simple miracles of Mother Nature."

It is common for bone marrow recipients to experience shortage of breath and pain in the liver and kidneys from the larger marrow cells entering those areas. I had some discomfort and some breathing difficulty, but compared with what I had already been through, this was mild. I began to feel a sense of confidence. *It can't get much worse than what I've already experienced,* I thought. Again I sought refuge in the practice of introspection and the teachings of Zen.

I stayed in bed most of that day, with my parents, Margaret, and a nurse at my side. Just after dinner that evening John was wheeled into my room. We both had tears in our eyes. Nodding my head, I greeted him with a simple "Thank you!" He nodded in acknowledgment.

There had been some complications in acquiring the marrow and the surgeons had had to cut John's tendons and muscles in the buttocks to get at his pelvis. The doctors originally told him that he would have trouble sitting for a few weeks, but after surgery he was informed that he would most likely experience more pain than anticipated. (He did indeed. When he visited me a few weeks later and I asked him how he was doing, he said, "Let me show you how much your brother loves you." He pulled down his pants to show me a backside black and bruised from his lower back down to his thighs.)

At 8:00 P.M. on the evening of the transplant, Zen centers in the United States, Canada, Poland, Sweden, and Costa Rica held chanting services directed to me. A group of prisoners in the state of Washington held a special ceremony on my behalf. My mother and sister also had several Christian services dedicated for my welfare at the same time.

I made my way from the bed to the large recliner in my room; it was the only time I would sit up that day. My family went into the waiting room to allow me some quiet time alone. Once the prayers and chanting began, I immediately felt as if I had tapped into a source of revitalizing energy. Strength returned to my body and I became aware of a deep peace. My hands kept floating up into gassho. Normally I do zazen with my hands in my lap. But after they floated up for the second or third time I decided that this was where they belonged. I had never before been on the receiving end of such a concerted effort on my behalf. Having now felt the penetrating power of these services, I can say with absolute certainty that chanting and prayers undeniably help beings who are suffering. When Sensei called later that evening from Costa Rica, she said my voice sounded so strong she thought I had not yet had the transplant.

As I sat, I felt connected to all beings who were suffering and I tried to reflect healing energy in their direction. It was too uncomfortable to think only of "taking" at a time like this. All beings were suffering, all beings chanting, all beings liberated; all beings were Buddha. I sat quietly, feeling waves of love and healing energy from so many people. I lost all sense of self. There was no birth, no death. For a while I disappeared. It was not until some time later, when the headaches and nausea returned, that I was forced to return to my bed.

It is impossible for me to describe the freedom and serenity that accompanied the ceremonies that night. I can only say that my heart was again at peace and full of gratitude. For me nights such as this remain among the fondest memories of my life.

Standing for a few moments, I faced the directions of several Zen centers and offered bows of gratitude. I went to bed that night after bowing to the altar in my room. I drifted off to sleep wondering what I had ever done to be so fortunate to have had so much spiritual help. My last thought of the day was, *How will I ever repay this enormous debt of gratitude?*

9

KANNON,
PLEASE HELP

I notice my withered form;
what can be done
for the rush
of this short scenario?
All night long
I cannot sleep.
Rising and sitting,
I think a thousand thoughts . . .
Only by observing
the state where there is no birth
can I remove these teardrops
from the wet sleeves of my robe.

—WEN-SIANG

"IF YOU NEED HELP, just ask Kannon. She will come to your aid." Sensei had said these words during one of my first retreats with her, and they made me uneasy. When the time came for private instruction, I charged into her room and said, "Fundamentally there is no separation. There is no self! Who is asking whom for help?" She looked me in the eye and said, "Jim, do you really think you can do this without help?"

I had been sitting zazen for many years when this encounter took place. During most of that time my practice had been based on self-reliance. One of the things that most attracted me to Zen was the aspect of depending upon oneself. Each of us had to do the work of awakening to our true Mind by ourselves; no one was going to do it for us. Only through perseverance and determination could we hope to come to the understanding of who and what we are. On his deathbed, the Buddha had said, "Be ye lamps unto yourselves." This appealed to me: relying on myself was a comfortable and familiar path. What I didn't see was that it was also a limited one. The Buddha's statement did not exclude asking others for help.

The challenges I had faced over the past six or seven months, and the love and support I had received, showed me that relying on others for help was an expression of oneness with all beings. When I asked for help I was living the truth of nonseparation. Zazen brought me glimpses of oneness with all beings. Illness was helping me realize that I was not alone.

While I could see this, I could not always integrate it into my everyday life. I understand now that asking for help when it is needed stems from our deepest wisdom. A yearning for assistance is a call from our mind of oneness, summoning us to look into who and what we truly are. Self-reliance is important, but there is no room for self-pride in spiritual practice.

The first week of March had arrived and I had not yet begun to experience the side effects of the radiation and heavy doses of chemo. I was scared. I knew I was coming into the worst part of my long treatment much weaker than I would have liked. I really had no idea how bad the side effects would be, but I did know that I was going to need all the help I could get. I vowed not to let my stubborn self-reliance make things more difficult this time around. Often when alone in my room I would think, *I'm only human. It's been a long haul and I've been through a great deal. I have to try to stay positive. Well, I'm doing the best I possibly can.* I had been warned well in advance that this might be the most difficult thing I'd ever have to face. *This is no time to be stubborn or proud,* I reminded myself.

Sometimes, before going to sleep, I would place my hands palm-to-palm and ask for protection. I knew for certain that my teacher would be there for me and there was no doubting the love and support of my friends and family. The terrible suffering soon to come could not be avoided. The only one who could really make things more difficult for me was myself. I prayed for humility and guidance to be able to see through my ego-delusion.

Periodically the hospital held orientations for bone marrow transplant patients to introduce them and their families to the hospital, its facilities, and the surrounding area. We had been unable to attend an orientation before my transplant because of my gallbladder surgery and lumbar puncture. The next orientation was the day after my bone marrow transplant, when I was in isolation. Margaret went while my mother visited with me.

As the meeting was closing, the social worker announced that they would be taking a tour of the BMT, Bone Marrow Transplant floor. Margaret told the group that her husband was one of the patients in the rooms they were going to visit. When she returned to my room, she said, "Jim, in just a few minutes there will be several BMT candidates and their families touring the halls. I told them it would be okay to meet you and ask a few questions."

"Well, make sure they start at the other end of the floor," I told her. "I need a few minutes to get ready." I looked like hell. *They will need encouragement,* I thought. *I don't want to look anything like that fellow I saw at St. Mike's trying to stand. Surely they are as afraid today as I was on that day.*

Because I was in isolation, no one from the group was allowed into my room, nor could I venture out into the hall. I did the best I could. Standing as straight as possible, I smiled, tried to look confident, and gave the patients-to-be and their families the thumbs up. It wasn't too hard to tell which ones were the BMT candidates; they were the men and women who were very pale and bald.

"Try to get out of bed every day even if only for a few minutes," I said. "For me, taking a daily shower is very revitalizing. If possible, bring a VCR and watch some movies, preferably comedies. The days, as you can imagine, do pass slowly. It's not that bad; you can do it. Many have before us. Let's keep in touch."

Margaret closed the curtain to my room. With IV pole in hand, I made my way back to the bed, making a mental note to be sure to remember my own admonitions. I was by no means an experienced BMT patient. My transplant had just taken place the previous day; I had not yet begun to face the effects of the more intense chemo and the radiation. Just the same, I was comfortable with having offered a few words of encouragement. I myself would have appreciated some positive words in the weeks before my ordeal. Margaret and one of the nurses later told me that many in the group felt more confident after having seen me so positive and "standing tall." I wondered whether I had led them astray. *Oh well,* I thought, *some worrying is inevitable. At least I didn't add to it.*

Throughout that week I washed quickly at the sink. Showering was far too tiring, and standing made my head throb. Fortunately, I did not have to shave: I had again lost all body hair.

During the next few days my headaches became more intense. A burning sensation developed in my palms and the bottoms of my feet. I began to vomit violently; the nausea was incessant. I didn't know if the vomiting was due to the terrible headaches or was from the effects of the chemo or the radiation treatments. It was probably a combination of all three. Whatever the cause, I hardly ate again for almost three weeks. I developed a fever. A rash began to spread over my torso and legs. I was in the thick of it.

Anyone who has had a serious flu—the kind where you ache in parts of your body you never knew existed and you're sure you're going to die—can begin to understand how one feels after intense chemotherapy. With chemo, though, the symptoms last for weeks and weeks on end.

My two most feared enemies were dehydration and infection. The doctors warned me that they could be hard to control once out of hand and often led to fatalities. My washroom had a bidet for sitz baths to cleanse myself thoroughly. Diarrhea was relentless and the sitz baths helped prevent infections, and they were a welcome comfort. To monitor dehydration, I was given three "hats" with measuring marks to keep track of output. The hats were half-moon shaped and had large, flexible rims so they could be placed on the toilet bowl to catch urine and bowel movements. One hat was also kept on the floor in front of the toilet to collect vomit.

On the morning of March 9 I was in the washroom vomiting when I heard Margaret greeting several people in my room. I finished up, washed, brushed my teeth, and had a sitz bath, wondering all the while what the heck was taking place outside the bathroom door. When I reentered my room, I found three smiling women from the kitchen staff. They carried cake, pastries, and fresh fruits and began to sing. It was our twenty-second wedding anniversary, and how they knew, I never did find out. As they left, they reminded us that I was not to eat any of the treats, since I was on a low microbial diet. Their songs and laughter brought some bright and positive energy into the room. All the same, it certainly didn't take much willpower for me to pass on the chocolate cake and strawberries. Margaret enjoyed the treats while I watched a children's television show.

When the doctors visited the next day, I told them about my continuing diarrhea and vomiting. They prescribed more anti-nausea drugs, including a drug derived from the marijuana plant. The nurses called it the happy pill, but I noticed no difference in my mental state. Despite the new drugs, the nausea and vomiting continued.

After lunch I felt quite low and asked Margaret to play a video

Amanda had made for me for Christmas. Randy was visiting, and as the three of us watched, I began to weep. Randy and Margaret asked if I wanted the video turned off. "Leave it on," I told them. "Even though it makes me feel very emotional and lonely for the children, it helps remind me why it's so important to keep fighting and to stay as positive as possible." It was a good cry, and soon I was out of bed doing yoga. I began a Sun Salutation stretch while Randy and Margaret looked on incredulously. "Well," I said, "you didn't expect me to go down without a fight, did you?"

My headache became worse whenever I stood up. Despite the discomfort, I decided to get out of bed every day and do some light yoga and Tai Chi. The workouts were only five to ten minutes long, but they gave me a chance to move my body and filled me with a sense of confidence. They also provided a much-needed break from the many hours spent on my back. Stretching and exercising were a way I met despair and discouragement head-on. Negative mind states only made my plight more difficult. I knew that a positive attitude would make all the difference in the world.

A few days later the doctors told me that the chemo they were administering that day might be the last one I'd ever receive in my life. Although the news was encouraging, the doctors also said that they were growing very concerned about my continuing headaches. "There may be some bleeding or swelling, or perhaps something else going on. We don't suspect it's serious at this point, but we'd like to do an MRI to be certain."

The Magnetic Resonance Imaging was painless though noisy. A few hours after the MRI, the doctor told me the test had revealed some swelling of the brain and meninges. He suspected I had leukemia of the brain and wanted to do a lumbar puncture to test for the presence of leukemia cells in the spinal fluid. I had suffered headaches from the lumbar puncture a few weeks earlier. About 20 percent of people having a lumbar puncture experience headaches because of a change in the spinal fluid. I was upset to hear that I would again have to have more fluid removed from my spine. The doctor informed me that the headaches I was presently experiencing were because of swelling of the meninges and not because of a change in spinal pressure. He told me that he would inject some saline solution into the spine after obtaining the sample. This, he hoped, would balance my spinal pressure and minimize the effects of the procedure. Of course, I was also worried about the possibility of having relapsed.

A lumbar puncture is quite painful under any circumstance. That day, moreover, the doctor ran into complications. As he inserted the needle, pain shot down my legs. It seemed that electric shocks were radiating from my spine through my buttocks and into my hips and thighs. I clung to my pillow, knuckles white, then began to grunt through clenched teeth.

Seeing my distress, the doctor apologized and told me he had hit a nerve and would have to start over. He then began the procedure again. After he had finished, he explained to the student doctor accompanying him what had happened and what to avoid. As I lay in sheets wet with sweat, the doctor said, "Jim, I'm sorry, but we won't know the results until tomorrow. I'll let you know as soon as I hear. I'm sure it won't be easy for you to get much sleep tonight. Ask the nurse for some sleeping pills if you need them." Once he got to the door he hesitated for a moment, then turned toward my bed and said, "Good luck, Jim. I hope things turn out okay."

I decided not to alarm my family until we knew the results of the test. Sensei called that afternoon, and we discussed my new dilemma. Randy, a few of my friends who had visited that day, Sensei, Margaret, and I all knew that we would just have to sit with this for a day or two.

After lunch that day Margaret went to phone her supervisor at work. When she entered my room, I could tell something was wrong.

"What's up?" I asked.

"Oh, it's nothing really. You don't need more to worry about."
She hung her head; her lips were pressed tight together.

"Margaret, please don't keep anything from me. It makes me
feel even more helpless. It's hard to explain, but being involved
with things that are happening at home helps me feel more alive.
There's not much left to the life I once had, hon. I can handle it,
whatever it is. We're in this together. Are the kids okay?"

"Oh, the kids are fine. It's just that, well . . . I think I just lost
my job."

"I don't believe it!" I placed my hands over my face. "Just when
I thought things couldn't possibly get worse. How the hell are we
going to feed the kids, Margaret? How are we going to feed the
kids?"

My disability insurance was covering all the household expenses, but we were depending on Margaret's wages to feed the
crew. With all we had to worry about, it seemed my mind was
most possessed with the financial problem.

"Well, I may still get work for a while yet," Margaret said. "My
supervisor tells me the union is going to negotiate for some of us
to stay on. I may get some shifts for a while. I have some seniority.
For goodness' sake, don't you worry about it. I'll find something."

I felt very sick for the rest of that day and, although I had eaten
nothing, continued to vomit small amounts of fluid and bile regularly. That evening I sat in bed for a long time not knowing if I
could make it to the toilet eight feet away. There was a large bowl
under my bed for emergencies, but that was of little use when I
was beset by diarrhea and vomiting simultaneously. I finally found
the energy to unplug my pump and make my way to the bathroom. Holding one hat to my mouth and placing the other in the
toilet, I began to vomit and have diarrhea at the same time. I took
note of the measurement in the hat I was holding and tried to
empty it into the toilet, but I had to remove the other hat first.
While struggling with the hat on the bowl, I tipped the one in
my hand, causing them both to spill. Margaret heard me swear in

frustration and went to summon a nurse. I could barely stand. I certainly wasn't well enough to be monitoring fluids and cleaning up after myself.

Margaret had become increasingly concerned with my continual vomiting and dry heaves. Never before had it been this severe. I looked at my reflection in the mirror. Green bile smeared my face and ran down my arm; diarrhea was spilled on my leg, foot, and the floor. The reflection staring back at me in the mirror looked feeble and emaciated. My heart rate had dropped to the low forties, my blood pressure was all over the map, and all attempts to keep me hydrated were failing. I knew I was close to death.

"Jim, do you want me to come in?" Margaret's voice came through the door.

"Please, and ask the nurse to come in as well, will you," I said. The nurse took one look at me and headed off to get drugs to stop the vomiting and help with the nausea. She knew that the dry heaves could cause internal bleeding and hemorrhaging when my platelets were so low.

As Margaret cleaned up the mess, I began to take off my pajamas. Although I had not bathed for three days and had only gotten out of bed to use the washroom, I decided to take a shower.

"Are you sure you're up to this?" Margaret asked.

"Margaret, before this past week, I never imagined one could feel so sick and still live. You know better than anyone what poor shape I was in before coming into this. But I have never felt this weak or this sick before. I may be going down, hon, but not like this." Looking at myself in the mirror, I thought, *You poor bastard.* I then threw the hats in the garbage and entered the shower.

The water on my face and back was refreshing. Standing in the shower I began to cry. *Is this what has become of my life?* I thought. *Measuring vomit and diarrhea? Damn! I'm too weak even to stand on my own.* With my forehead pressed against the shower wall for support, I stood for a long time sobbing.

Leukemia of the brain? What does that mean? Weeks to live? Days? What types of treatment can kill off the fast-growing leukemia cells in the brain and at what cost? I knew of only one person, younger than I, who was being treated for this. After they had drilled a hole in his head, inserted a shunt, and begun the treatments, he lost more than a hundred pounds and was still confined to a wheelchair.

Will I be able to do zazen after all this? What quality of life can I expect? Will I opt to have the treatment? I wonder if we'll have to sell the house? How are we ever going to buy groceries? There's no way I can keep facing these emotional challenges and not break sooner or later. Is there no end to this? Or maybe this is how it's going to end. I've led a good life. Surely I'll be reborn into favorable conditions. Death would be far easier than what I'm going through now. . . .

For goodness' sake, man, pull it together! You know where this can lead. Enough! Enough of that. Things will work out. You've never been a quitter. You've come too far to give up now.

Standing in the shower with cool water running on my face, I focused on my breathing and forced myself to inhale and exhale slowly and deeply. I turned down the hot water slightly. The cooler water was invigorating. I felt life and energy seeping back into my body and light coming into my heart and mind. When I left the shower, I looked at the pathetic figure in the mirror and said to myself, *Don't give up! Stay with it, kiddo, this fight's not over yet!*

Margaret, looking worried, pointed to the toilet bowl and to the flourescent green bile I had vomited up. Margaret and I both said how pretty it was. I don't think I had ever seen such a pretty green.

"You'd better get a nurse to look at this," I said. "It doesn't look good." My bowel movements, too, were green.

The nurse told us that after heavy doses of chemo this was not uncommon, but we should definitely continue to notify her of color changes. The colors of bowel movements and vomit indicate many things about a post-BMT patient's condition.

From that night on, I no longer measured my fluid output in hats. The nurses were adamant that I should continue using the hats, but I didn't have the strength to do so. Instead, I marked approximate amounts on a chart on my bathroom door. It was a compromise I could live with. After a day or two, the nurses accepted my solution. Really though, I gave them little choice.

Late that night, alone in my room, a deep cry for help arose within me. Once again I was facing despair and depression. *Leukemia of the brain? No food for my kids. I don't believe this. There's no way I can handle any more of this. Man, it sure seems like I've been in the hospital for a long time facing one hurdle after another. This might be it. Perhaps the time has come to say good-bye. If I'm not ready after all this, I'll never be ready. What lies ahead? Death maybe, more suffering for sure, financial problems, and if I'm lucky, perhaps some good days. Where is that light at the end of the tunnel I've heard about?*

I raised the bed, turned to face the altar in my room, and, holding hands palm-to-palm, prayed for help. Although I desperately wanted to be well, this prayer was for guidance. *Great bodhisattvas, I need help! Kannon, please help me! Please help me find the courage, the strength, and the power of concentration to see through my dilemma.* Soon I disappeared into my yearning for help.

What kind of help am I looking for? Who is it who calls out to whom? An opportunity presented itself to look into these questions in a way not ordinarily possible.

My situation compelled me to look into my impulsiveness, my fanaticism, my self-confidence, and my stubborn self-reliance. As I looked intently, I was called out of my guts and into my heart. Somehow I knew that this was possible only because of my heart's opening to help from others.

I began to fall. But unlike the heavy sinking sensation I had experienced over the past few months, it was a buoyant feeling of release and letting go. My body felt weightless and unburdened. An unraveling began in my chest as if a large knot were becoming undone, and I merged into the One Mind of all beings. Tears of joy ran down my face and soaked my gown. *This is impossible,* I thought. *How is it that during the most difficult time of my life I can be so full of joy and gratitude?* Whether I lived or died seemed to matter little. In my true Self there was neither birth nor death. *All things in the* universe are none other than my own Mind. *Indeed, the universe unfolds as it should.*

I got out of bed and faced the altar on the window ledge and made a standing bow. I then turned in the direction of the Toronto Zen Centre, the Vermont Zen Center, and other centers and offered more bows of gratitude. *How fortunate I am to be alive!* I was so happy to have found the Buddha's teaching and felt so blessed to be dealing with my illness in this way. *Gratitude tonight? I can't believe it. Well, what better way to prepare myself for the many mind states I might encounter after death?*

The next morning Ian and Margaret came to visit. Although the last night's experience had brought me great peace, I was again feeling nauseated. I fervently hoped that I would not have to undergo chemotherapy treatments to the brain. The day passed slowly. Just before dinner the test results came back: the swelling was due to an allergic reaction to an antirejection drug. There was no leukemia in the brain or nervous system. Hearing this, I broke into tears. Ian, Margaret, and I embraced each other. I immediately called Randy and asked him to call Sensei to let her know the good news. I also asked him to offer incense for me before the Kannon at the center. My heartfelt gratitude was due not only to the results of the test. The previous night's experience had so filled me with light and peace that I had no room in my heart for anything but gratitude.

Although I had not eaten much in weeks, I ordered blueberry pie and ice cream to celebrate and managed to eat most of it. That night some friends joined Margaret and me for a video. We ate popcorn and had sodas. We all felt immensely relieved and grateful that I would not have to go through another round of treatments.

Later that day, Margaret told me that Sunyana-sensei had asked her permission to start a "Bedard Family Fund." A notice was put in sangha newsletters and we began receiving food and monetary gifts from several different Zen centers. Margaret and our children were delighted and touched to see the boxes of food delivered to our house. Over the next year, we also received checks totaling many thousands of dollars. My whole family was awed to see the extent to which we were helped by the small sanghas in Toronto, Vermont, and elsewhere.

For the next week the terrible headaches and nausea continued. My lower back and neck became inflamed and there was a great deal of pain in my kidneys. Just the same, the days went by. Ian, Ross, and Randy visited every day, read to me, and helped me pass the time. Margaret, family, and friends were constantly at my side. Sensei visited every time her busy schedule brought her to Toronto.

The drugs sometimes made me delirious. One afternoon when Sensei was visiting, I began to pass out. I was receiving platelets and was given the usual drugs to help prevent the rigors. Earlier that day I had also been given some antirejection drugs and antinausea drugs. The combination caused me to become intoxicated. I woke up hearing someone talking in my room and realized it was my own voice. I wasn't making any sense at all, but was greeted by a sweet smile from Sensei. I tried to explain but again could make no sense. "It's okay, Jim," she said, "you don't have to talk. We can just visit in silence." Which we did.

The next few weeks were filled with terrible flulike symptoms, head and ear pain, vomiting and diarrhea. As trying as that was, I began to notice the "X" marks on the calendar getting wonderfully close to the week Mike had pointed to on the day I had been admitted. From time to time I was able to get a meal down and could drink more fluids. Soon there were periodic moments of feeling well that seemed to grow every day.

About five weeks after being admitted to Princess Margaret Hospital for the transplant, I was discharged to the lodge. Staying nearby allowed me to visit the hospital daily. It was at this time that I felt most out of touch with everyone. There were constant problems with incoming calls. I had to wander to the end of the hall on the next floor to make any outgoing calls. Despite these inconveniences, I was stronger than I had been in weeks and was thus able to sit in a chair and do zazen. I set up an altar in my room and took the Three Refuges. I did zazen and chanted almost every day.

I began coming home for weekends and then for longer periods. On my first afternoon home I walked the neighborhood with Brad accompanying me. I staggered as I walked. It had been so long since I had been outdoors that the clouds and sky mesmerized me. "Dad," Brad said, "you're acting just like a kid. You keep stopping to look at the flowers and the trees." He found it quite amusing to see me so immersed in the walk. Never again can I take a simple walk on a spring day for granted.

Once I was strong enough to travel, Randy, Ross, Ian, and I went to our cabin for a weekend. The hills seemed steeper and the walks were shorter than usual. Just being there with the guys made me realize once again what a precious thing this life is. I felt so fortunate to be alive. We sat on the front porch in silence and watched the sun set as we had done a year ago. This time we were more aware of the evanescence of life. It had been quite a year.

Late that August, Margaret and I had a gathering at our home in Bethany to show our appreciation for the love and support we had received. It was one year since I had been diagnosed with AML leukemia. My mom was there to fulfill her promise: "You'll make it, son, and in a year's time we'll have a party to celebrate." Friends and family joined us for the occasion. When the meal was over I presented the group with a large cake. On it was a picture of two hands palm-to-palm and the words "With deepest gratitude for your love and support."

10

NURTURING
THE SELF

> May all beings be happy.
> May all beings be well.
> May all beings find peace.

ADJUSTING TO HOME LIFE was difficult. Although I no longer had the energy or strength I once had, somehow taking off my pajamas and putting on normal clothing caused me to revert to old habit patterns and push myself too hard. I had difficulty finding a balance between activity and rest. Moreover, some of the drugs I was taking gave me a false sense of energy.

That summer I developed a terrible headache that lasted five weeks. I spent many hours late at night walking circles in our kitchen with my hands pressed to the sides of my head. Several times I had to call for emergency assistance. A second time the doctors thought I had relapsed and had leukemia of the brain. An MRI showed swelling and I underwent another lumbar puncture. Naturally, I was concerned about having relapsed, but I didn't allow myself to get too upset. I had learned not to worry needlessly—things might turn out okay. Instead, I used the time during the test to look into suffering, its cause, and freedom from suffering. The test was negative.

A month later I was in North Bay when the specialist called from Princess Margaret Hospital. A third time they suspected leukemia of the brain. More tests. Negative. The doctors now suspected the head and ear pain were from an ongoing allergic reaction to one of the antirejection drugs I had been on months before. To counteract the allergic response, I was given steroids. This seemed to help the pain but made me irritable and restless.

The debilitating headaches continued and made it impossible to sit upright and do formal zazen. However, through the last year I had learned to practice mindfulness while lying down. This, as well as a special practice Sunyana-sensei gave me, helped me find peace and some relief from the pain in the midst of it all. Unfortunately, when I didn't have the energy to carry on this practice, the headaches returned. Finally I visited a neurologist, who immediately pinpointed the problem. I was indeed having an allergic reaction, not to one of the antirejection drugs, but to codeine. I continued with my special practice and discontinued the codeine, and within a week my headaches had all but disappeared.

In early September, about six months after my transplant, Margaret and I were given the opportunity to join my parents for a trip to see the Rockies. I was nervous about traveling for days on end in a car and concerned about being so far away from the hospital. As well, since I had been on disability for more than a year, we didn't have money for a vacation. Margaret and I vacillated about going. My friends, family, and Sensei, however, had no such reservations. They urged us to take the trip, as they felt it would help my recovery and be a welcome change for Margaret. Finally they convinced us to go.

When I went for my biweekly checkup just before we left, I asked my doctor what she thought of my traveling so far. She said, "Jim, I think you should wait until you have a few more months under your belt before making such a demanding trip."

"Doc," I told her, "already two of the people I usually see at clinic have died. A few others who had their bone marrow transplants when I did have relapsed. Do you think I should wait until I'm sixty-five and retired to make the trip out West? I've always wanted to see the Rockies."

"Well, if you put it that way, Jim, what choice do I have?" she said. "We can give you the names of the bone marrow transplant clinics in all the major cities from here to Vancouver. You will be only a phone call away. So, have a pleasant trip. But be sure to be back before a month is up. It is very important that we continue to treat your lungs with antibiotics and that you have your blood checked regularly. Your health is still very fragile."

It was a magnificent trip. We spent a couple of nights in Banff, visited Lake Louise, and traveled along the coast, stopping often to see the sights. The contrast between being closed in for so long in my hospital bed and seeing the mountains was overwhelming. I now understand where the expression "It took my breath away" came from. Although I had to spend a day at the clinic in Calgary and was sick for a couple of nights, for the most part my health was not a problem. Resting in the car, I took in the mountains with reverence.

We stayed with Eric and his wife, Linda, in Victoria. One night we were their guests on the S.S. Beaver, a paddle boat that tours Victoria's harbor, for an evening show featuring Eric's impressive magic. Eric and Linda took us through the rain forest on the north end of Victoria Island. We visited Cathedral Grove—a stand of pine trees several hundred years old—and even saw some whales.

It was a wonderful break. We came home refreshed and grateful. We were fortunate, too, that my parents and the sangha had helped pay for the trip.

One of the many challenges of long-term illness is financial. We now faced car repairs, replacing a kitchen window, and kids who needed new clothing and shoes for school. We were broke and in debt. To make ends meet, we decided to sell our camper. (No, not to my brother John.) We also renegotiated our mortgage. Margaret found part-time work as a dietary aid. Still, it was going to be tight—many of the household expenses were not being met. Once again the sangha stepped in to help. We also received monetary gifts from close friends, family, and my colleagues at work.

A few weeks before our Jukai ceremony at the center, we had a sangha meeting. When the time came for suggestions and comments, I told the group, "When I was diagnosed just over a year ago, Margaret and I had no idea there would be many other challenges we would have to face. The food drive, the monetary offerings, and your love and support over the past year have made this whole ordeal so much easier on my family and me. Thank you so much—I could not have done this without your help."

In early October I asked to meet with Sensei. I did not have to remind her that more than a year had passed since I first asked to become her disciple. Again I made the request. After this long, trying year, we had gotten to know each other well.

She said, "If you still wish to make this commitment, we can do the ceremony when I am in town next month for Great Jukai."

The sangha spent many weeks preparing for Great Jukai. Great Jukai is held only once every three years and differs from the normal yearly Jukai. The Zen center was decorated from top to bottom, each room adorned creatively to represent the six realms of existence. We were guided through the house, visiting each of the different realms. After our trek through the hell, hungry ghost, animal, titan, human, and deva realms, we entered the Buddha Hall, which symbolized our having found the dharma. Once seated, everyone took the precepts. I felt so thankful to be practicing again, to be at Great Jukai, and to be taking the precepts as a disciple of Sunyana-sensei.

Earlier that day Sensei had helped me fulfill my earnest wish.

In a simple, private, and deeply moving ceremony, I became her disciple.

Normally at this ceremony a disciple makes a monetary offering to his or her teacher, but Sensei would have none of it. Although she had a gift for me, she had made me promise not to make an offering. She knew how difficult our financial situation was, and she preferred that I keep the money for my family.

The day after Jukai, when I was about to leave the center for home, I visited Sunyana-sensei and again asked if I could make even a small donation. "You know, Sensei, for thousands of years students and disciples have made donations to their teachers as a way to demonstrate their support for the teacher's dharma work. Surely you won't stand in the way of such a wonderful tradition." Sensei again refused. But just before I left for Bethany, she said to me, "You know, Jim, there is something you could do."

"Please, Sensei, just name it," I said, feeling relieved that she might be offering me a way out of my dilemma. "You know I feel deeply indebted and need to express my appreciation for all the support and guidance you have given me over the past year. I'm sure you are aware that I'm looking for a way to express my heart-felt gratitude for having become your disciple."

"Well, Jim," she replied, "why don't you write something about your experiences over the past year. You could write a book about the way you have dealt with your illness. It would be very helpful to others."

That night at home, after sitting in zazen, I did a chanting service and offered incense. As I made my final bow facing the Buddha figures on my altar, I thought of that first night when I had returned home from the emergency ward in Peterborough with swollen hands and ankles. *I am so grateful to have been able to take refuge in the Buddha's teachings,* I thought. *So grateful to have had so much support. We can't escape the ripening of past karma but we can choose how we want to deal with it. How will I ever repay this enormous debt of gratitude?* I then placed my hands palm-to-palm and vowed to write this book.

A week later, as I was awakening from my afternoon nap, an

extraordinary thing happened. I entered a state of consciousness such as I had never experienced before. Someone so earthy, so grounded that I thought she was Mother Earth herself stood behind me. Her palms rested on my forehead and her fingers cradled my head. As she touched me, I felt a golden light entering my body. It was painful, yet strangely wonderful at the same time, and I knew it to be a healing energy. The light ran throughout my nervous system, down my spine, and into my arms and legs. I placed my hands on top of hers to let her know that it was okay to continue. I began to sob from the marvel of it all and said aloud, "It's okay. It's okay." I had complete trust in this healer and the energy that was radiating throughout my body. I felt so nurtured, so loved, and so protected that I knew that regardless of whether I lived or died, I was being healed.

Margaret opened the door to our bedroom and asked, "Who are you talking to?" I opened my eyes and saw that I was alone.

"Margaret, the strangest thing just happened. I hope you don't think I'm going nuts." I then told her about the golden light. "Perhaps my body is trying to tell me something, but I'm not sure what it is. . . . Margaret, I think I've just been cured." Then I noticed the time.

Many of my dharma brothers and sisters were in sesshin in Vermont. What I had experienced had taken place during the afternoon chanting service. It was obvious that many of my dear friends were focusing their energy on me during that time. Still, I had to wonder who their messenger had been. Could a bodhisattva have responded to their appeal?

A week later when sesshin had ended, Sensei called. I told her what had happened and she said, "Jim, it was a wonderful sesshin. Several of the participants told me in private that they were dedicating their efforts to your well-being. There was a great deal of merit being sent your way." My experiences over the past year left me with no doubt that what I had experienced that afternoon and many other times was indeed due to the efforts of others practicing with me in mind.

In early October, about eight months after my transplant, Margaret and I had stopped in to see the nurses on the seventh floor and in the ICU ward at St. Michael's Hospital. We brought some treats and thank-you cards as an expression of our gratitude. I was saddened to learn that my friend with AIDS had died. I also found out that the handsome young doctor with the fancy silk ties was now married. I was not surprised.

That night I did some light stretching. I even managed to do ten push-ups, not minding at all that I was slowing considerably on the last few. I then walked a mile or two. It was a beautiful fall evening, and as I ambled through the neighborhood, I noticed the full moon appearing on the horizon. The cool fall air filled me as I walked slowly through our small town.

A poem by James Wright that Randy had recited to me while I was ill came to mind:

> As the plump squirrel scampers
> Across the roof of the corncrib,
> The moon suddenly stands up in the darkness
> And I see that it is impossible to die.
> Each moment of time is a mountain.
> An eagle rejoices in the oak trees of heaven,
> Crying
> This is what I wanted!

I would have to write a separate book to express the gratitude I feel to all those who have helped make this ordeal so much easier for my family and me. May the balance of this life provide me with an opportunity to repay their benevolence in some small way. Margaret and our children, Sunyana-sensei, my parents, my siblings and their families, my dear friends and the Zen Buddhist community—all have given so freely and selflessly that I will be forever filled with gratitude.

AFTERWORD

SEVERAL MONTHS after this book was written Sunyana-sensei journeyed to Japan on pilgrimage. When she returned I was astonished to learn that my story was not yet finished.

While in Japan Sensei went to many Buddhist temples and was able to fulfill one of her lifelong dreams—she visited Sanjusangendo, a revered national treasure in Japan. It is a large hall that houses one thousand and one figures of Kannon, the Bodhisattva of Great Compassion. Sensei said that when she finally arrived there, she was so overcome with emotion that for more than an hour she could not speak. Knowing that I also have deep-seated affection for this bodhisattva, my teacher presented me with a booklet of this celestial site upon her return.

I was delighted to see the images of the elegant carvings of Kannon. As I leafed my way through the pictures, I was suddenly awestruck. I had turned a page and found a picture of a life-size carving of "an old man wearing a brown tunic deliberately leaning on a staff." I immediately recognized him as the old man I had seen when my consciousness left my body on the day I was dying in ICU. There was absolutely no doubt in my mind. I called Sensei at once and told her to look in the booklet. She too recognized him straightaway from the description I had given. Tears of gratitude came to my eyes as I began to realize what had actually happened on that afternoon. How fortunate I am to have met a bodhisattva in my time of need. They do indeed respond to our cries for help.

There is an inscription under the picture of the twelfth-century carving that introduces the bodhisattva. His name is Basusennin (also called Vasu). He is a Buddhist hermit who continually goes on pilgrimage through the wilderness saving beings who have lost their way. The booklet from Sanjusangen-do explains: "He is a lonely and unworldly man in appearance owing to his strict religious practices in pursuit of Buddhistic truth and charity." I have also learned that he is most often accompanied by men and women he has saved from the hellish realms, some of whom I saw on that day. Vasu is familiar with the after-death state and guides lost souls to a place where the Buddha's dharma is being practiced. He too must have been responding to that cry for help I heard and found me there, lost and confused. He then ushered me to a Buddha realm. I can hardly believe that I thought he had come to me for help. It is understandable, though, since he really did not fit my image of a bodhisattva.

Now I understand his look of compassion, his sense of confidence, and the light of wisdom that shone from his eyes. I also appreciate why he did not enter the Buddha realm that I found myself in. And I know now why he was smiling. Should you have the good fortune of meeting him someday, know that his name is Basusennin and he is a friendly and loving soul. I am certain I will meet him again.

BASUSENNIN
(*Artist: Steve Spring,*
Toronto, Ontario, 1998)

CHANTS

The Four Bodhisattvic Vows

All beings, without number, I vow to liberate.
Endless blind passions, I vow to uproot.
Dharma gates, beyond measure, I vow to penetrate.
The Great Way of Buddha, I vow to attain.

The Three Refuges

I take refuge in Buddha, and resolve that
with all beings I will understand the Great Way
whereby the Buddha seed may forever thrive.

I take refuge in Dharma, and resolve that
with all beings I will enter deeply into the sutra-
treasure whereby my wisdom may grow as vast as
the ocean.

I take refuge in Sangha, and in its wisdom,
example, and never-failing help, and resolve to
live in harmony with all sentient beings.

The Three General Resolutions

I resolve to avoid evil.
I resolve to do good.
I resolve to liberate all sentient beings.

THE TEN CARDINAL PRECEPTS

I resolve not to kill, but to cherish all life.

I resolve not to take what is not given, but to respect the things of others.

I resolve not to engage in improper sexuality, but to lead a life of purity and self-restraint.

I resolve not to lie, but to speak the truth.

I resolve not to cause others to take substances that confuse the mind, nor to do so myself, but to keep my mind clear.

I resolve not to speak of the faults of others, but to be understanding and sympathetic.

I resolve not to praise myself and disparage others, but to overcome my own shortcomings.

I resolve not to withhold spiritual or material aid, but to give them freely where needed.

I resolve not to indulge in anger, but to exercise control.

I resolve not to revile the Three Treasures—Buddha, Dharma, and Sangha—but to cherish and uphold them.

ZEN MASTER HAKUIN'S CHANT IN PRAISE OF ZAZEN (Zazen Wasan)

From the beginning all beings are Buddha.
Like water and ice, without water no ice,
outside us no buddhas.

How near the truth yet how far we seek,
like one in water crying "I thirst!"
Like a child of rich birth
wandering poor on this earth,
we endlessly circle the six worlds.

The cause of our sorrow is ego delusion.
From dark path to dark path

we've wandered in darkness—
how can we be free from the wheel of samsara?
The gateway to freedom is zazen *samadhi*—
beyond exaltation, beyond all our praises,
the pure Mahayana.

Observing the precepts,
repentance and giving,
the countless good deeds,
and the way of right living
all come from zazen.

Thus one true samadhi extinguishes evils;
it purifies karma, dissolving obstructions.
Then where are the dark paths that lead us astray?
The pure lotus land is not far away.

Hearing this truth, heart humble and grateful,
to praise and embrace it,
to practice its wisdom,
brings unending blessings,
brings mountains of merit.

And if we turn inward
and prove our true Nature—
that true Self is no-self,
our own Self is no-self—
we go beyond ego and past clever words.

Then the gate to the oneness
of cause and effect
is thrown open.
Not two and not three,
straight ahead runs the Way.

Our form now being no-form,
in going and returning we never leave home.

Our thought now being no-thought,
our dancing and songs are the
voice of the dharma.

How vast is the heaven
of boundless samadhi!
How bright and transparent
the moonlight of wisdom!

What is there outside us,
what is there we lack?

Nirvana is openly shown to our eyes.
This earth where we stand
is the pure lotus land,
and this very body, the body of Buddha.

PRAJÑA PARAMITA HRIDAYA (HEART OF PERFECT WISDOM)

The Bodhisattva of Compassion
from the depths of prajña wisdom
saw the emptiness of all five
skandhas and sundered the bonds
that create suffering.

Know then:
Form here is only Emptiness,
Emptiness only form.
Form is no other than Emptiness,
Emptiness no other than form.
Feeling, thought, and choice,
consciousness itself,
are the same as this.

Dharmas here are empty;
all are the primal void.
None are born or die.

Nor are they stained or pure,
nor do they wax or wane.

So in Emptiness no form,
no feeling, thought, or choice,
nor is there consciousness.
No eye, ear, nose,
tongue, body, mind;
no color, sound, smell,
taste, touch, or what the mind
takes hold of,
nor even act of sensing.

No ignorance or end of it,
nor all that comes of ignorance:
no withering, no death,
no end of them.
Nor is there pain or cause of pain
or cease in pain or noble path
to lead from pain,
not even wisdom to attain,
attainment too is Emptiness.

So know that the bodhisattva,
holding to nothing whatever
but dwelling in prajña wisdom,
is freed of delusive hindrance,
rid of the fear bred by it,
and reaches clearest nirvana.
All buddhas of past and present,
buddhas of future time,
through faith in prajña wisdom
come to full enlightenment.

Know then the great dharani,
the radiant, peerless mantra,
the supreme, unfailing mantra,
the Prajña Paramita,

whose words allay all pain.
This is highest wisdom,
true beyond all doubt,
know and proclaim its truth:

Gate, gate
paragate
parasamgate
bodhi, svaha!

TEN-VERSE KANNON SUTRA

Kanzeon!
Praise to Buddha!
All are one with Buddha,
all awake to Buddha—
Buddha, Dharma, Sangha—
eternal, joyous, selfless, pure.
Through the day Kanzeon,
Through the night Kanzeon.
This moment springs from Mind.
This moment itself is Mind.

EN MEI JIKKU KANNON GYO

Kanzeon!
Namu Butsu
Yo Butsu U In
Yo Butsu U En
Bup Po So En
Jo Raku Ga Jo
Cho Nen Kanzeon
Bo Nen Kanzeon
Nen Nen Ju Shin Ki
Nen Nen Fu Ri Shin

MEDITATION CENTERS

Toronto Zen Centre

33 High Park Gardens
Toronto, Ontario M6R 1S8
Canada

Phone: 416-766-3400
Fax: 416-769-4880
Email: tzc@interlog.com
Web site: http://www.interlog.com/~tzc/

Vermont Zen Center

37 Thomas Road
P. O. Box 880
Shelburne, Vermont 05482-0880
USA

Phone: 802-985-9746
Fax: 802-985-2668
Email: vzc-graef@worldnet.att.net
Web site: www.vzc.org/

NOTES

1. Zen retreats, or *sesshins*, are three- to seven-day periods for the intensive practice of Zen meditation. Participants meditate for ten or more hours a day, eat simple vegetarian meals, and receive instruction in Buddhism.

Chapter 1: Letting Go

1. A large wooden block that is struck with a mallet to announce the beginning of rounds of meditation, or zazen.
2. The historical Buddha, Siddhartha Gautama, or Shakyamuni Buddha, was born 2500 years ago. His teachings are known as the "Middle Way" of Buddhism. A buddha is anyone who has completely freed himself or herself from all attachments and attained enlightenment. The Buddha is not a god but is recognized as a teacher of eternal truths.
3. Chanting, or liturgical recitation, is one of the essential practices of Zen Buddhism and is another type of meditation. Scriptures are chanted in a low monotone accompanied by the sonorous tones of large bowl-shaped gongs, *keisu*, and the constant beat of a wooden drum, *mokugyo*.
4. Buddha figures represent our true Mind—the Mind of perfection, wisdom, equanimity, love, and compassion—which is innate in all creatures. Looking at the countenance of such figures, and bowing and prostrating before them, is a way Buddhists remind

themselves that they, too, have the capacity to manifest these virtues.

5. The law of cause and effect, or karma, states that what we sow, we shall reap. Karma is not the same as fate. A person's karma is created by the person's own intentional actions in lives from the distant past through the present moment; it is not determined by an outside power. One can accumulate "good" karma from helpful and loving actions, which leads to meritorious effects, or "bad" karma from pain-producing actions, which leads to painful effects. All causes (or karmas) produce effects that will be experienced in one of three periods of time: the immediate present, sometime in the present lifetime, or in a future life. In order to expiate negative karma, there must be an acquiescence in whatever one is experiencing, a recognition of one's responsibility for the situation, even though one likely does not remember what one did to cause it. (This does not mean, however, that one should have a placid acceptance of the misfortunes of one's life. If you can change something, do so. That, too, is your karma.) A belief in karma presupposes an acceptance of the doctrine of rebirth, since it is impossible for all karmic effects to come to fruition in any one lifetime. Karmic "debts" impel a person to be reborn. Karma is so complex that it is symbolized in Buddhism by an endless knot.

6. Dharma refers to the teachings of the Buddha and the spiritual path of Buddhism. This saying means that if you practice the teachings of the Buddha with sincerity and devotion, no matter what happens, you will be strengthened and supported by them.

7. Bodhisattvas are beings of compassion and wisdom whose purpose in life is to bring an end to suffering. Practitioners of Zen Buddhism try to develop the virtues of the bodhisattva. To this end they make four bodhisattvic vows: to liberate all sentient beings; to uproot endless blind passions; to penetrate innumerable dharma gates; to attain the Great Way of Buddha.

8. The room used for Zen meditation, or zazen.

9. *Sensei* and *Roshi* are honorifics. *Sensei* means "teacher" in Japanese and is used for younger Zen teachers. Roshi means "venerable teacher" and is the title of older Zen teachers.

10. In Buddhism, *ego* refers to a sense of oneself as being a distinct entity, separated from and confronted by a world one mistakenly

perceives to be outside oneself. The ego, or small self, is that which obstructs our ability to see our true Self, which is not apart from the universe.

11. The Three Refuges, or Three Treasures, are the common denominator of all forms of Buddhism. To take refuge means to put one's trust in the ideal of an enlightened being (Buddha), in the teachings of the Buddha (dharma), and in the community of those who practice the Buddha's dharma (sangha).

Chapter 2: Facing Death

1. Sutras contain the teachings of Shakyamuni Buddha. The *Diamond Sutra* is one of the most important texts for Zen Buddhists.
2. A type of Buddhist rosary carried by many Buddhists.
3. A short chant dedicated to Kannon, the Bodhisattva of Compassion.

Chapter 3: Starting Over

1. In Buddhist cosmology, there are six unenlightened realms of existence, which can be understood literally or metaphorically: those of heavenly beings (*devas*), power mongers (warring titans), humans, animals, hungry and thirsty ghosts (*pretas*), and hells. Beings in the realm of the hungry ghosts suffer from unquenchable thirst and ravenous hunger. Although there is food, they are unable to eat; it turns to poison. Although there is water, they are unable to drink; it turns to fire. It is said that these pitiable beings have condemned themselves to this existence because of their insatiable, blind greed in previous lives.

Chapter 4: Karma

1. Canadian Thanksgiving is in October.

Chapter 6: The Faith to Doubt

1. A Caribbean dish: flat bread rolled around various savory foods.
2. Jukai is the most essential ceremony of the year for Buddhists. It involves the formal taking of the Three Refuges, the Three General Resolutions, and the Ten Cardinal Precepts (see chants).

Upon participating in a Jukai ceremony, one officially "enters the Buddha's family." Zen Buddhists attend Jukai at least once each year.

Chapter 7: Visiting Other Realms

1. Philip Kapleau, *The Wheel of Life and Death: A Practical and Spiritual Guide* (New York: Doubleday, 1989), 120.

ACKNOWLEDGMENTS

FIRST AND FOREMOST, I would like to express my profound gratitude to my teacher, Sensei Sunyana Graef. I will be forever grateful for her guidance and loving support. From the book's inception through to its completion, she worked tirelessly assisting me. She demonstrated the patience of a bodhisattva as I found my way through the trials and tribulations of writing a first book.

Thanks also to Holly Callery for working with us for many hours editing the manuscript and for making many helpful suggestions. I would also like to thank my agent, Susan Cohen from Writers House; my editor Emily Hilburn Sell; and my friends at Shambhala for all their assistance.

I am most grateful for the love and support I received while I was ill, from my wife, Margaret, and our children; my parents, siblings, and extended family; my dear friends Ian Henderson, Ross Gray, Randy Baker, and many others. I feel deeply indebted to my dharma brothers and sisters; they have assisted my family and me in innumerable ways. I am particularly grateful to my first Zen teacher, Roshi Philip Kapleau; his letters and words of encouragement helped me face this whole ordeal with newfound courage and determination. I feel inexpressible gratitude toward all these people for their continuous support through the recent difficult but enlightening years.

I wish to send a special thanks to my donor, my brother John. Thanks also to the medical doctors, nurses, technicians, and hospital staff who made this journey back to health possible, and to all who prepared meals for me while I was on an almost impossible diet.

I would like to express my deepest gratitude to all those who have helped me sustain my spiritual practice for many years. I prostrate before buddhas and bodhisattvas who guide and aid us in inexpressible ways. Thank you Basusennin for helping me find my way when I was lost.

May all beings find peace.
January 8, 1998